RONALD KERSHAW AND
BRIAN ROBSON

Discovering Walks in the Cotswolds

SHIRE PUBLICATIONS LTD.

CONTENTS

The maps were drawn by Richard G. Holmes.

Copyright © 1974 and 1976 by Ronald Kershaw and Brian Robson. Number 191 in the Discovering series. ISBN 0 85263 646 6. First published 1974. Second edition 1976. Reprinted 1979. Third edition 1983.

INTRODUCTION

This book has been written for people who would like to go walking in the Cotswolds and wish to avoid the roads. Some people are unaware of England's marvellous system of footpaths; many know the footpaths are there but are unable or disinclined to seek them out for themselves. One way of getting to know the paths is to join one of the local rambling clubs but this may not always appeal and is impractical for the holiday walker. This book, then, is an introduction to walking in the Cotswolds for visitors and those who wish to walk alone or in small groups.

Ten routes are described in detail; with one exception there is at least one shorter version so that the length of the walk may be selected to suit one's tastes and abilities and the time at one's disposal. For timing it is reasonable to assume a speed of two miles an hour. The walks are distributed over the whole area of the Cotswolds and many famous beauty spots are visited.

The Cotswolds lie mostly in Gloucestershire. They are roughly contained by a line joining Cheltenham to Bath, then running east to Oxford, north to Banbury and back through Evesham to Cheltenham. The only towns are Cirencester and Stroud, though there are a number of large villages. The characteristic feature of the area is the underlying Cotswold limestone, a wonderful yellow stone used to build the Georgian towns of Bath and Cheltenham but equally effective for mansions, churches, houses, farms or barns. It is difficult to think of an ugly building in Cotswold stone, still less a village.

Cotswold stone is porous, so streams always seem small in relation to valley size. There are no great summits to be scaled but a day's walking can be quite energetic. In Walk 6 for instance, there is a total ascent (and descent) of 2,000 feet, which is rather more strenuous than climbing one of the Three Peaks.

In the Cotswolds there are numerous small villages, many of which have both a church and an inn. As the Ordnance Survey maps do not always indicate the presence of the latter this information is included where necessary in the descriptions. The OS Landranger 1:50,000 series (1¼ inches to 1 mile) shows public rights of way where available. Four sheets are required to cover the area of the walks, numbers 150, 151, 162 and 163. If you intend doing much walking in the area, the 2½ inch (1:25,000) maps are invaluable as they show field boundaries, but unfortunately rights of way are not shown on the current series. Every endeavour has been made to use rights of way and we have tried to select only those paths easily negotiated by unskilled ramblers. Nevertheless paths may become overgrown, ploughed up, muddy or obstructed and you must use your own discretion in dealing with such drawbacks. A pair of secateurs and a walking stick can be useful.

The countryside is the farmer's workshop and as such it is by no means static. New farmhouses and barns are built, farm layouts modified, fences and hedges removed, occasionally the latter being replaced by fences. Sometimes stiles are replaced by gates or the line of a path is altered slightly to suit the convenience of the farmer. The felling of trees removes landmarks but opens up new vistas. So the walker should be prepared occasionally to find the countryside not quite fitting the details given and must then use a little ingenuity to discover the route.

Key to the locations of the walks in this book.

Circular walk from Broadway to Snowshill and Stanway returning via Stanton, Laverton and Buckland (10½, 8½, or 4 miles).
1-inch map no. 144; 2½-inch map sheet SP 03. 1:50,000 map no. 150.
Buses from Evesham.
Car parking in Broadway and on Broadway-Cheltenham road (A46) near Buckland and Laverton.

The walk climbs the Cotswold escarpment and goes by lane and path to Snowshill, then across the wolds and through woods to Stanway, the seat of the Earl of Wemyss. Parkland paths then lead to Stanton, a lovely village, after which field paths are taken to Laverton, Buckland and back to Broadway.

The walk may be shortened by omitting Stanway and further shortened by taking paths direct to Laverton.

BROADWAY. This is a popular village with shops and cafes around the village green. The parish church is along the Snowshill road, but a much older church (St Edburgh's) stands about three-quarters of a mile along the same road. It contains a brass to Anthony Daston (1572).

The walk starts from the village green at **Broadway** by following part of the Cotswold Way, a long-distance footpath that runs from Chipping Campden to Bath. Go along the Snowshill road towards the parish church. 50 yards past the church turn right down a lane to enter a field through a small gate near the end of the lane. Cross the field to a footbridge, then aim for a gate ahead some 100 yards to the right of a house, a stile by the gate giving access to a minor road. On the opposite side, 10 yards to the right, is a stile. The path climbs the field, bearing away from the hedge on the left, to a stile 50 yards to the right of the field corner and entering a wood. After about 20 yards a junction of paths is reached. Take the left-hand path climbing and winding through the wood for 250 yards to a hunting gate and entering a field with a hedge on the left. Keep along the hedgeside and through a gate ahead. Go forward some 30 yards, then turn right downhill for 40 yards and over a cattle grid to a farm road. Turn left through a gate, bearing right to go along a fairly straight track for three-quarters of a mile. Note Broadway Tower on the hill across the fields to the left. Ignore an entry into farm buildings halfway along the track. Go through a gate beyond which the track divides. This is where the shortest route diverges (1).

If one of the longer walks is being undertaken, the route now leaves the Cotswold Way, but this will be walked again later. At the gate above go forward, ignoring paths on the right, with Buckland Wood on the left. Near the top of the hill views over

Buckland to Bredon Hill may be seen by looking back. Continue through two gates, then turn right on a good farm track with a wood on the right. In about half a mile the buildings at Little Brockhampton will be seen over on the left and in another half-mile the few houses at **Great Brockhampton** are reached. Keep to the track to the right of the buildings until just beyond the houses a left U turn is made. 30 yards down the track a footpath starts by a gate on the right, descending with a valley on the left, then continuing to a hunting gate near an electricity pole. Go forward for 50 yards, then bear right with trees on the right, to go through a gateway. Continue bearing right round the shoulder of a hill (ignore paths to farm buildings on the left) and down to an inconspicuous gateway on to a track. Bear right along the track which climbs and leads to a road where a left turn brings the walker to **Snowshill.**

SNOWSHILL is tucked away in a combe below Oat Hill. The houses are arranged round the village green with a cross and the church at one corner. The church is nineteenth-century with a font from an earlier church and a Jacobean pulpit.

The Manor, owned by the National Trust, is a mainly Tudor house with a front dating from about 1700. It contains collections of musical instruments, toys, bicycles and tools. The house is open to the public at certain times.

Refreshment may be obtained at the Snowshill Arms.

Leave Snowshill along the road by which you entered, passing the track up which you came. At the first road junction take the right fork. Ignore the next road on the right but turn left along the next track. In the field on the left is a group of round barrows, one of which yielded a dagger now in the British Museum. Views across to Oat Hill are seen on the left. After some 300 yards farm buildings will be passed on the left. Go through the iron gate ahead into a field, alongside a wall on the left and bearing left. After 100 yards go through the gate ahead, bearing right alongside the remains of a wall on the right for 400 yards to come out through a gate at a junction of roads and tracks. Turn right through a gate with a wood on the left. You are entering the Stanway Estate and the path is marked by posts with *red* tops. Continue up the right-hand field boundary for 700 yards, climbing gradually until a cross-track is met. Here go forward, with a wall and trees on the right, to a wood. At this point there are a number of notices to read. The shorter route diverges here **(2).**

For the longest walk turn left along a track marked by posts with *green* tops. After 250 yards go down the track by a notice, ignoring the track to the barn on the left and the gate on the right. The track descends through a delightful mixed wood, all paths to right and left being private and so marked. Look out for pheasants

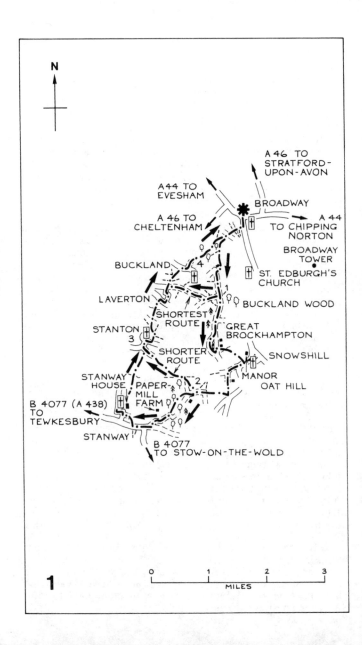

1

N

A 46 TO STRATFORD-UPON-AVON

A 44 TO EVESHAM

BROADWAY

A 46 TO CHELTENHAM

A 44 TO CHIPPING NORTON

BROADWAY TOWER

BUCKLAND

4

ST. EDBURGH'S CHURCH

LAVERTON

BUCKLAND WOOD

1

SHORTEST ROUTE

STANTON

3

GREAT BROCKHAMPTON

SHORTER ROUTE

SNOWSHILL

STANWAY HOUSE

PAPER-MILL FARM

MANOR OAT HILL

2

B 4077 (A 438) TO TEWKESBURY

STANWAY

B 4077 TO STOW-ON-THE-WOLD

0   1   2   3
MILES

among the trees and for wild flowers. In just over half a mile the
wood ceases on the right and the track rises, with fields and a
valley on the right. Across is seen Papermill Farm, a typical
Cotswold farm backed by meadows and woods, and on the site of
an old paper mill. The track leads to the Tewkesbury to Stow-on-
the-Wold road (B4077). Go forward down the road to **Stanway.**

After about 500 yards, a signposted path will be found on the
right. Enter through a gate, bear right in front of cottages on the
left to go through a gate and along a track leading to a road where
a right turn brings the walker to the gatehouse at Stanway House.
(Alternatively, the main road may be followed to crossroads where
a right turn by the war memorial will lead to the gatehouse. This
route passes the Old Bakehouse where refreshment may
sometimes be obtained.)

STANWAY. The manor-house is the seat of the Earl of Wemyss and
is built of Cotswold stone. The house and gardens with the
gatehouse and church make a delightful picture. The
gatehouse is seventeenth-century; the identity of the architect is
uncertain though the building has often been attributed to
Inigo Jones.

The church was built in the twelfth century but much restored
at the end of the nineteenth century. The tithe barn, of cruck
construction, was built in the fourteenth century for the Abbot
of Tewkesbury. It looks more like a church than a barn. It is not
open to the public except when functions are held there.

From Stanway to Stanton the Cotswold Way is followed. From
the gatehouse follow the road to Stanton and go past the
entrance on the right to Stanway House grounds and tithe barn.
150 yards beyond, a stile and signpost on the right indicate the
start of the path to Stanton. Cross the field half-left to a stile over
an iron fence and go in the same direction for 200 yards to cross
an avenue of trees. After passing a barn on the left, go to a gate
in the fence parallel to the avenue and near the corner of the
field. The path crosses the corner of the next field to a gate.
Through the gate cross the field on a line approximately parallel
to the fence some 40 yards to the left, aiming at a solitary oak
tree, then look to the left of the oak tree ahead for a derelict
footbridge and awkward stile. Now cross the field bearing
slightly right to a farm gate. The path goes through two fields on
the left of the hedge and enters over a stile a few yards to the left
of the gate. Follow the field edge with the hedge on your right.
Cross the next field to the right-hand end of the iron fence
ahead, turning left through a wooden gate at Chestnut Farm. Go
down the lane, then right to the road at **Stanton**, going forward
to the main street of the village.

STANTON is one of the loveliest of small Cotswold villages, with its cross on a medieval base. Old barns have been converted into modern dwellings. The church is part Norman but has been altered over the years. It contains fifteenth-century glass, said to come from Hailes Abbey.

The Mount Inn, where refreshments may be obtained, is reached by keeping left at the top of the village street.

(3) Leave the village by going up the entry by the cross to the church. Enter the churchyard on the left and immediately go round this right-handed to the far corner. Here a path goes right between two walls, then a wall and iron railings. At the end of this path ignore the obvious stile ahead but turn left between railings to go through a swing-gate and over a small footbridge. Keep to the hedge on the left for 100 yards and as the path bears right go over a stile in the hedge on the left.

Continue along the side of four fields with the hedge on the right. In the fourth field is a stone stile about 15 yards to the left of the field corner and, on going over, the hedge is now on the left. Keep to this hedge and in the corner ahead cross a small footbridge and go over the fence. Cross the fence on the left some 10 yards ahead to go alongside the field boundary on the right and out of the field by a stile just to the left of the field corner, on to a road. Turn right, then left at the first junction to the village of **Laverton.**

Follow the road through the village and on coming to a T junction notice an entry ahead. This leads to a good path between hedges which brings the walker, without difficulty, to a road, where turn right to the village of **Buckland**. As you go up the road note the first metalled lane on the left (after about 100 yards) to which you must return to continue the walk.

BUCKLAND is another lovely village with old cottages and colourful gardens. The church dates from the thirteenth century and is of great interest. The font is fifteenth-century and very ornate. There are ancient pews and wainscoting. On the north wall is a piece of fifteenth-century embroidery on blue velvet. The manor-house stands near the church. It is worthwhile walking to the top of the village to look down the road to the church and cottages.

(4) Go along the metalled lane mentioned above, which bears right passing cottages on the left. At the end go through a small wooden gate, then slightly right to a stile and ahead for 50 yards to another stile. Keep to the hedge on the left for some 20 yards, then bear right, climbing steeply a short distance to two oak trees. The path now climbs slowly towards a wood on the right and continues round and below the base of the wood. It then bears right, on an

even contour, across a clearing to enter a wood through a hunting gate. Go forward on a good path which winds along the edge of the wood for 600 yards before coming to a junction of a number of paths. You have now completed the circuit and will retrace your footsteps to Broadway. Go over the stile ahead, then down to the stile in the field corner. Cross the minor road, go over the stile just to the right and across the field to the footbridge and small gate ahead. Continue up the lane, turning left at the road to arrive in **Broadway.**

The shorter route (8½ miles)

Follow the main route to the end of the paragraph marked (2).

Go through the large wooden gate ahead and down the track for 300 yards to a gate into a field. Continue alongside the wall on the right. Just before the corner of the field is reached there is a wooden hunting gate on the right. Go through, turn left along the wall side which bears left below a wood to a wooden gate on the brow of the hill. Go through this and across the field half-right on a path going through a gap in the hedge approximately halfway up from the lower field corner. At the gap bear slightly right across the field to go through a narrow belt of trees on a track and through a gate. 100 yards beyond this, ignore a track going right into a valley, but go forward down the track to a gate with a wall on the right. The track goes down through two fields to a wooden gate at Chestnut Farm, the buildings being on the right of the gate. Go down the lane, turn right to the road at **Stanton**, continuing forward to the main street of the village.

Now continue the walk from the paragraph marked (3) in the main route.

The shortest route (4 miles)

Follow the main route to the end of the paragraph marked (1).

Continue on the Cotswold Way by turning right beyond the gate previously mentioned, bringing a hedge on the right. The track leaves the hedge, bearing left to go through a gate. The track now bears right, then left, and after about 250 yards passes through the remains of an old gateway. In a further 150 yards it goes through a gate, climbing towards some trees. At the trees a sunken path occurs on the right. Now leaving the Cotswold Way, turn right down this path, which after 150 yards turns left through a gate. Hereabouts extensive views are obtained across the valley. The track is level for a short distance then bears right descending the hill to go through a gateway. Here ignore the track to the right, but go down a sunken path which leads to a metal gate. Continue down the field towards the village of **Laverton**, the path leading to a gate with a stream on the left. Go through the gate to reach a metalled road, going down until a road comes in on the left. Immediately on the right is an entry. This leads to a good path between hedges which brings the walker without difficulty to a road, where turn right to the village of **Buckland**. As you go up the road note the first metalled lane on the left (after about 100 yards) to which you must return to continue the walk.

Now continue the walk from the paragraph marked (4) in the long route.

Walk 2   **OVER BREDON HILL**

Circular walk from Bredon's Norton over Bredon Hill to Ashton-under-Hill returning via Woollas Hall (12, 8, 5, or 4 miles).

1-inch map no. 144. 2½-inch map sheet nos. SO 93, SO 94. 1:50,000 map no. 150.

Buses from Cheltenham, Tewkesbury and Worcester (very infrequent).

Park cars in or near Bredon's Norton or Ashton-under-Hill. Bredon's Norton is just off the Tewkesbury-Pershore road, B4080.

From Bredon's Norton the walk goes up the western slope of Bredon Hill, (an outlier of the Cotswolds), and gives extensive views across the Avon valley to the Malvern Hills. The route crosses the top of the hill to the eastern side, giving views across the Vale of Evesham to the Cotswolds, then descends to Ashton-under-Hill. The return is made along the north-east slope on to the northern escarpment with views to Pershore and northwards, then descends to Woollas Hall and back to Bredon's Norton.

The walk may be shortened by omitting Ashton-under-Hill and further shortened by not crossing the Hill. A short walk from Ashton-under-Hill is also described.

BREDON'S NORTON is an unspoilt village at the western foot of Bredon Hill. Parts of the church date from the twelfth century but the nave was rebuilt in 1886 after a fire. The tower has a two-dialled clock. The manor, which you will pass, is sixteenth-century and at the front is an archway dated 1585, with fine iron gates. The owner in those days, Sir Thomas Copley, is said to have sailed to America with Sir Walter Raleigh. To the left of the manor is the fourteenth-century tithe barn, said to have been used by William Shakespeare for his plays. At present there is a stage at one end.

Behind the manor, on the hill, is Norton Park, built in 1830 on the site of an earlier house.

From the school at **Bredon's Norton**, on the corner of a T junction, go up the road with the church on the left. At the top

turn right along a lane signposted to Bredon Hill. On the left along
the lane are the tithe barn and the Manor House. After 100 yards
turn left and in 50 yards go through a small iron gate on the left of
the track and up to farm buildings. Turn right and at the end of
the buildings turn half-left across a field for 100 yards to double
gates (one behind the other). The track winds up the hill. In the
trees on the left is Norton Park. In 600 yards go through double
gates but ignore the gate on the right. The path continues winding
upwards for 400 yards to another pair of gates. The track now
bears right towards a small barn which is passed on the right
(ignore the track going left before reaching the barn). The track
continues climbing slowly and bears left to a gate into an old
quarry. Do not go through but turn left up a path which winds
round the quarry to come up to a terrace on the edge of a field.
Turn left on the terrace which bears right, round the field. In some
500 yards a wall comes up on the left as the path bears further
right and in 40 yards go through a gate in this wall on the left. Go
ahead on a well-defined path which winds over hummocks, with
an old quarry on the right, to a line of trees. Go through a gate at
the trees and turn left along a good track with trees on the left and
a fence on the right. The shortest route diverges here **(1)**.

In 250 yards go through a gate on the right and immediately
turn left through a gateway, then turn right alongside the wall and
trees on the right. After 200 yards pass a small wood on the right
and go forward towards farm buildings, then bear left to go
through a gate. Cross in front of a barn to a track. Ignore a gate on
the left just past the buildings and follow a good track through a
gate and along the side of a field with a hedge on the left. In 350
yards, at the field corner, turn left over a stile and up a track with
a wall and belt of trees on the right. After 250 yards, at the corner
of the wood, turn right along a track with the wood on the right. In
300 yards cross a metalled lane and go forward for 700 yards on a
winding metalled lane. Where this turns sharp left up to a mast,
go ahead, with a fence and wood on the right, for about 600 yards
to meet a cross-track. Turn left up the track for 200 yards to go
through a gate and across a narrow field, then through another
gate on to a track by a line of trees. The shorter route diverges here
by turning left **(2)**.

(3) Turn right on a good path, with trees on the left and a fence
on the right. 250 yards past the end of the trees go through a gate
and forward with a wall or fence on the left. There are now extensive views across the Vale of Evesham towards Stratford-on-
Avon and the northern end of the Cotswolds. After continuing on
the path for 450 yards, ignore a gate on the left and in a further
200 yards go forward through a gate. Where the path bears right,

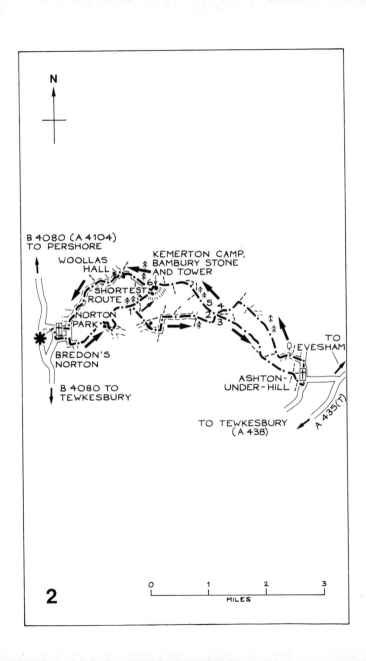

N

B 4080 (A 4104)
TO PERSHORE

WOOLLAS
HALL

KEMERTON CAMP,
BAMBURY STONE
AND TOWER

SHORTEST
ROUTE

6

NORTON
PARK

5

1

2

3

BREDON'S
NORTON

TO
EVESHAM

B 4080 TO
TEWKESBURY

ASHTON-
UNDER-HILL

TO TEWKESBURY
(A 438)

A 435(T)

2

0   1   2   3
MILES

ignore a small gate in a dip on the left. Continue until, on the left,
the end of the wall is reached and there is a steep bank.

Here turn right alongside the fence on the left for 20 yards and
go through a gate on the left. Go down the track ahead which in
200 yards divides. Take the right fork and in 20 yards go through a
gate. Now turn half-left across the field, passing a small enclosure,
to a gate in the hedge ahead which at first is concealed from view.
Through the gate turn right down the field with a hedge on the
right, bearing slightly left to go over a stile 30 yards left of the
corner, then across a field and over the stile ahead. Now aim just
to the right of two trees some 400 yards away. At the trees bear
slightly right to the hedge and go down the field side. Ignore a
track going left halfway down the field. At the bottom cross a
track and go through the gate ahead. Now go just to the right of
the church below, passing a pond on the right and down a
metalled path with the church on the left, into the road at **Ashton-
under-Hill.** Turn left along the road to the Star Inn where
refreshment may be obtained.

ASHTON-UNDER-HILL. Most of the houses of the village are along a
single street and consist of thatched black and white, Cotswold
stone and brick buildings. It is very pleasant to walk up the road
looking at the cottages and gardens.
The church is one of the few dedicated to St Barbara. St
Barbara is said to have been beheaded by her father for
becoming a Christian and he was later killed by lightning.
Hence St Barbara became the patron saint of blacksmiths,
firearm-makers and artillery. She is depicted in the east window. Parts of the church are very old, though additions have
been made over the years. The font is fourteenth-century.
Outside the church is the village cross, believed to date from the
fifteenth century.

From the Star Inn turn left up the road and left along Cottons
Lane (the second road on the left). The lane winds uphill for 500
yards to the entrance to Shaw Green. Ignore the gate on the right
and go up the drive. Where this turns left to the house, bear right
uphill, then through an iron gate at some trees and up a narrow
track. After 100 yards, at a Y junction, take the right fork. In 300
yards at a junction of tracks (there is a water-trough on the left) go
straight ahead to an iron gate into a field with a hedge on the
right. Keep to the hedge for 500 yards, with woodland and a deep
valley on the right (ignore gates into the wood), to reach an iron
gate. Continue for 300 yards with the wood on the right to a
hunting gate near the corner of the wood (horse jump to right of
gate). The path bears left and then passes through a group of trees
and goes over a cross-track, with cattle pens on the right. Go

through the right gate of two in the field corner beyond the pens, into a field with trees on the left. Ignore a gate on the left, but go ahead, crossing a boggy patch, passing a derelict barn on the left and up to a gate. Through this go ahead across the field for 300 yards to the far boundary. The mound half-right is the site upon which Elmley Castle once stood. Turn left up the boundary of the same field to a small gate by tall trees. Keep ahead through the trees for 100 yards, the path emerging on to a track. Turn half-right along the track for 200 yards until a wide track comes in on the left. Cross this and turn half-right up a narrow path through a wood and out on to a track, there being a gate opposite the path, through which you came on the outward journey. Turn right along a good path **(4)**.

(If you are returning to Ashton-under-Hill go to the paragraph marked (3) but turn left instead of right.)

(5) After 300 yards go through a gate into a field with a fence on the right. On the left is the mast previously seen. After 600 yards ignore a gate and track on the right but go forward with trees on the right. In 150 yards the path passes between trees to a gate. Continue for 500 yards on a good path (ignore the path going down right) to go through a gate with a wall on the right and in 250 yards another gate. After passing on the left the double earthworks of **Kemerton Camp** make for the tower.

KEMERTON CAMP AND BAMBURY STONE. This Iron Age camp dates from about 100 B.C. and covers some 22 acres. It has two ramparts.

In a hollow north of the tower are fragments of the Bambury Stone, once on the edge of the hollow. The use to which this stone was originally put is a matter of conjecture.

The tower (sometimes known as Parsons' Folly) was built by a Mr Parsons in the eighteenth century as a summer-house or lookout tower and of such a height that the top would be 1000 feet above sea level (the hill is 961 feet high).

There are extensive views northwards of the villages of Eckington and Pershore and the winding river Avon.

(6) From the tower, look for a stile in the wall below, slightly to the right. Go over and descend the steep hillside very carefully (avoid the well-worn paths and use the grass at the side; the right-hand side is probably the easiest). At the bottom go on a visible path over hummocky ground, bearing left, then down to go through stone gateposts in a cross wall. Continue bearing left for 30 yards, then bear right so that in 100 yards there is a small wood on the right. Go down the hill, passing a spring on the left, to a stile by an iron gate. Continue down for 200 yards to join a good track. 100 yards down this go through an iron gate. Here turn half-

left across a meadow to a stile on to a metalled drive, turning left
to **Woollas Hall.**

WOOLLAS HALL was built in 1611 by John Hanford on the site of
the former Manor of Wollashull. He died in 1616 and is buried
in an elaborate tomb in Eckington church. Various members of
the family lived in the hall until 1938, but it is now divided into
flats. There is a Jacobean staircase leading to the many panelled
rooms.

Go over the cattle grid and along the drive with the hall on the
right. The drive winds between delightful houses and gardens,
then becomes a track. 200 yards past the next cattle grid and
after passing a house on the left, the track turns right (ignore the
gate ahead) to an iron gate. Follow the track round farm
buildings, continuing as the track winds through fields for half a
mile to an iron gate. Here a metalled road starts, which in three-
quarters of a mile leads to **Bredon's Norton**. In the village turn
right at the first junction and left at the next, to reach the point
from which you started.

Shorter walks

Shorter walk from Bredon's Norton (8 miles and nowhere for
refreshment)
   Follow the walk to the end of the paragraph marked (2), then
continue from the paragraph marked (5) in the long route.

Shortest walk from Bredon's Norton (5 miles)
   Follow the walk to the end of the paragraph marked (1).
Continue with a fence on the right for a quarter of a mile. Then
the path bears left and shortly right for 100 yards through trees to
a gate into a field with a wall on the left. Keep to the wall and in
400 yards go through a gate and continue along the path to the
tower. Now go to the paragraph marked (6) in the long route.

Short walk from Ashton-under-Hill (4 miles)
   Follow the route from Ashton-under-Hill to the end of the
paragraph marked (4) but turn left instead of right. Now go to the
paragraph marked (3) in the long route.

Walk 3   **OVER CLEEVE HILL**

---

*Circular walk from Prestbury over Cleeve Hill to Winchcombe
   returning via Belas Knap (11, 8, 6½, or 4 miles).
1-inch map no. 144. 2½-inch map sheet nos. SO 92, SP 02.
   1:50,000 map no. 163.
Local bus service from Cheltenham. No. 587 to Prestbury and
   Cleeve Hill. Castleway bus service Cheltenham to Winchcombe.*

Also service 527.

Car parks at Cleeve Hill and Winchcombe. Car parking in Prestbury is permitted in the Kings Arms car park out of licensing hours, so that motorists are advised to start at Cleeve Hill or Winchcombe.

The walk starts at the Prestbury war memorial and local bus stop, climbs the escarpment to go over Cleeve Common, passing through Postlip to Winchcombe. The return is made via Sudeley, Wadfield and Belas Knap to Cleeve Common and Prestbury.

The walk may be shortened and climbing reduced by starting at Cleeve Hill bus terminus or car park and still further shortened by omitting Winchcombe and returning via the 'Washpool' and Cleeve Common.

The walk may be started at Winchcombe going via Belas Knap to Cleeve Common and returning via Cleeve Hill or the 'Washpool'.

The walk affords magnificent views over the surrounding valleys.

From the **Prestbury** war memorial leave the main road (A46) and go along The Bank, the road behind the memorial, for 100 yards to a T junction where turn right to the A46. Turn left along this for 120 yards, then cross to a stile under a tree with a signpost 'Southam and Cleeve Hill'. Go half-left across the field to a stile some 60 yards to the right of a house, to enter a lane. On the opposite side a few yards to the left is a lane. Go along this for 250 yards. Where the lane turns right, go ahead over a stile adjacent to an iron gate, then bear slightly right across a meadow to a wooden fence and stream. Cross carefully, then turn up the field keeping near to the hedge on the right. Go over a stile between two trees in the fence ahead. The stile is end-on to the path and not easily seen. Now bear left to go up beside a wood on the left for some 600 yards. The path is well defined initially, then crosses a boggy patch and becomes less clear. Continue beside the wood, ignoring gates into it. At the top of the field, turn right, with trees on the left, to the corner of the field where there is a wooden hunting gate. Go through, over a small stream and a covered strand of barbed wire just beyond the gate. Continue upwards, keeping close to the hedge on the left. After about 250 yards, ignore a hunting gate on the left but continue upwards for another 100 yards, then bear right towards a belt of trees to join a track, some 80 yards right of the field corner, going through the trees. The track bears left, then right, and in 150 yards a cross-track is met, where turn left uphill. Ignore side tracks and in 100 yards the track bears left. Ignore the stile in the wall on the right but keep along the track, making for a gate 200 yards ahead giving access to Cleeve

Common. Keep ahead, with a steel fence and wall on the left until the main track is reached. Continue on this track but ignore the one going down leftwards where the fence ends. 30 yards from this you will reach a group of trees known as 'The Three Sisters' (there are now only two).

(1) Ignore the track going right but go forward, up and down over old earthworks for 100 yards on the edge of the escarpment. There are now extensive views. Note below the brow of the hill a square stone block—Huddlestone's Table, where the King of Mercia said farewell to his guests who had been to the dedication of Winchcombe Abbey. Now bear right on a good path away from the escarpment towards a golfers' sighting pole (an iron mast) 200 yards away among Iron Age earthworks. The path bears left, then forward for 600 yards with the escarpment on the left. Note the triangulation point ahead with the tracks leading up to it; this is where you are heading. The left-hand track is the one you will use. The path now rises over Cleeve Cloud, the cliffs on the left being a mecca for rock-climbers. Over the brow the path descends for 100 yards to a Y junction.

Take the track going right, soon crossing over a track coming up from the left, and go between hummocks ahead. Ignore a path going right. Pass a tee on the right, then go over a cross-track towards a putting green ahead. On the left are two tracks. Take the one uphill towards gorse bushes and leading to the triangulation point, near which is a topograph giving distances to and sketches of prominent landmarks.

Go round the right-hand side of the putting green, then between two tees to turn left along a good track with a fairway on the left. After 400 yards the track bears left to a gravel track with a building on the left. Go forward on this track, noting Bredon Hill ahead on the horizon. The track bears right and about a quarter of a mile away will be seen the club house to which you are going. On reaching this turn right, passing the end of a metalled road on the left. Now go to the paragraph marked (2).

From **Cleeve Hill** bus stop and lower car park go through a small gate and straight ahead for 100 yards up a rough track, then turn left round a house and stables. Go up a track with an iron fence on the left for 100 yards to bring the golf course on the right. Go forward for a quarter of a mile, passing in turn on the left an old quarry, the club house and the end of a metalled road.

(2) You are now on a good path with a fairway on the right and a wall on the left. In 600 yards go through a wooden gate and in 400 yards through another gate and forward for 10 yards to a junction of tracks. Turn half-right down a track towards trees, leading in 100 yards to a cross-track.

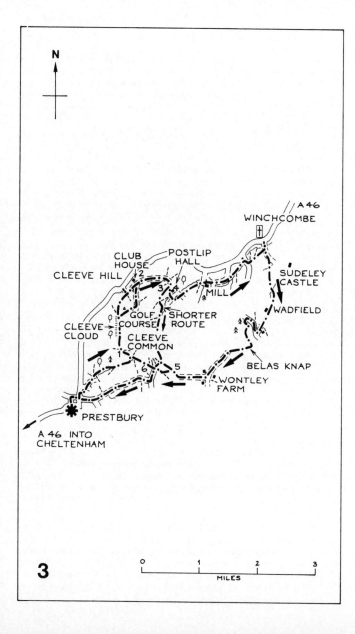

N

CLEEVE HILL

CLUB
HOUSE

POSTLIP
HALL

WINCHCOMBE

A 46

SUDELEY
CASTLE

MILL

WADFIELD

GOLF
COURSE

SHORTER
ROUTE

CLEEVE
CLOUD

CLEEVE
COMMON

BELAS KNAP

5

WONTLEY
FARM

6

PRESTBURY

A 46 INTO
CHELTENHAM

3

0   1   2   3

MILES

The shorter route from Prestbury and Cleeve Hill via the 'Washpool' diverges here **(3)**.

(4) Go over the track and forward to pass through an iron gate between trees, the path skirting the wall of **Postlip Hall** on the left. In 200 yards, as the track bears left, go through another gate and over a farm track. Ignore the entrance to the hall on the left and keeping the wall on the left pass through a smaller gate, the ground hereabouts being muddy at times. Bear left along the track with the wall of the hall on the left, aiming for a gate on to a cross-track. On the left is an entrance to Postlip Hall. Immediately opposite the gate is a stile with a notice 'Public Footpath to Winchombe'. This gives access to a path which may be overgrown. In about 80 yards go over a stile, past a barn on the right, and over another stile into a field with a hedge on the left. In 700 yards cross an old stone slab bridge on the left, a few yards before reaching the lower field corner (crossing the infant river Isbourne). Over the bridge turn right to a gate and forward to Postlip Mills, where special papers are made.

Go ahead towards 'Reception' and as the works road bears left, turn right past the fire station on the left, then bear left under a covered way and straight ahead between buildings to a lane. Ignore the road on the left and a track on the right. Go ahead for half a mile. At a gateway the lane bears left and later, where it turns sharply left and uphill, look for a stile on the right. Go over this into a field with a fence on the right and a large house on the left. In 250 yards go over a wooden stile and across a field to go through a gate near the right-hand field boundary, then straight ahead to a stile and gate leading to the Cheltenham-Winchcombe road (A46). Either go forward along the main road to the centre of Winchcombe or turn right up a minor road (signposted to Brockhampton and Belas Knap). In 200 yards where the road turns right, go through a gate on the left, ignoring the stone stile to the left of the gate. Go alongside the hedge on the left. After 300 yards the path becomes enclosed by a hedge and fence, leading to a stile into a field with a hedge on the right. Go ahead and through a gate into the road at the entrance to **Sudeley Castle.** You will return to this point to continue the walk. Turn left for the centre of **Winchcombe**. On the right as you go up the road are old almshouses.

WINCHCOMBE is an ancient Saxon burgh, but the abbey, which was once of great importance, was so effectively destroyed during the Dissolution that no traces of it remain. The stone was no doubt used locally, possibly in the building of Sudeley Castle. The oldest parts of Winchcombe are the fifteenth-century church of St Peter and the George Hotel which was built by the abbey as an inn for pilgrims. Many of the houses in the High

Street, including the Old Corner Cupboard inn, date back to the sixteenth century.

SUDELEY CASTLE dates from the fifteenth century and has had a chequered history. It was much restored during the nineteenth century and is now frequently open to the public. There are the remains of a royal suite of rooms, one of which is known as Queen Catharine Parr's room. She was Henry VIII's widow and married Lord Seymour in 1547, but she died a year later.

To continue the walk, retrace your steps to the entrance to Sudeley Castle, but follow the road as it bears right at the entrance. In 300 yards, where the road bears left, turn half-right through a kissing gate and along a path signposted Belas Knap. Follow the direction of the sign arm over a slight rise to an electricity pole and down a dip to cross a wooden stile and a stream by a stone slab. Continue in the same direction for 300 yards keeping left of a clump of trees, and making towards an electricity pole with glass insulators some 30 yards right of a gate. Here there is a double stile and between them a metal footbridge giving access to a field with a fence on the left. Cross this diagonally for 300 yards, aiming for a point some 200 yards right of the far left-hand field corner to cross a stream by a wooden bridge. Go forward with a fence on the right for 100 yards, then turn right and go over a stile. Turn left, climbing steeply with trees on the left, to reach a hedge ahead. Turn right alongside the hedge, climbing steadily. In 200 yards go over a stile by a gate and in a further 200 yards go through a gate to the left of the house at **Wadfield.** ('Wadfield' is a corruption of 'woad field'; years ago woad was grown hereabouts for the dyeing industry.) The path keeps to the left of the farm buildings for 200 yards. The way is now well defined and can be seen continuing to rise and bear left for 500 yards, then turning right to pass to the right of Humblebee Cottages. Go forward for 100 yards to the Winchcombe-Brockhampton road.

Turn right along the road for 500 yards, noting the view on the right of Winchcombe and Sudeley Castle. At the Belas Knap sign turn left, climbing for 100 yards through a wood to go through an iron swing gate into a field. Turn left, keeping to the field boundary, first on the level, then turning right and climbing steadily. (Look back as you rest, for views over Winchcombe to the Vale of Evesham.) In 400 yards go through another swing gate, turning left and keeping to the hedge and wall on the left. After 400 yards go through a wooden gate and over a stone stile to arrive at **Belas Knap**. You will continue the walk in the direction in which you are now going.

BELAS KNAP is a Stone Age burial mound, 180 feet in length, which has been carefully preserved by the Department of the Environment. There is a false entrance at the north end; there are three burial chambers, one with an entrance on the west, the other two with entrances on the east.

Leave the barrow by the stone stile opposite the one by which you came. Keep to the right of a long field and in 700 yards turn left along a track for half a mile to the old buildings of Wontley Farm. Here turn right by the building on the right and continue up a straight track with a fence away to the right. In 300 yards the path leads to a gate and in a further 500 yards to another gate **(5).**

Through the gate turn half-left on a path. Once more you are on Cleeve Common and at the top of the rise you will see the radio masts. The path leads to a broad track (note the triangulation point ahead by the wall); turn right for 150 yards to a Y junction where bear left on a path to the radio masts.

(6) To return to Prestbury

Leave the Common through a wooden gate and go along the metalled lane which goes towards a wood. Ignore the first path on the right but bear right on a path near the wood and which descends to the side of the wood. At this point the path may be soft underfoot but lower down a bank on the left may be used as the path. Keep going down the main path, ignoring side tracks and in 500 yards the path becomes a metalled lane. Follow this for three-quarters of a mile, then go over a cross-road and straight ahead for 500 yards to the main road (A46). Cross and go forward to the first junction, where turn left to the war memorial and bus stop at **Prestbury.**

(6a) To return to Cleeve Hill

At the radio masts turn right along a broad track with a wall on the left for half a mile, passing a group of trees on the left. Soon there are extensive views over Cheltenham. At a second group of trees on the left ignore a gate at a signboard and in 200 yards ignore the track going down at the end of the fence on the left. 30 yards from this you will reach two trees on the right, known as 'The Three Sisters'.

Ignore the track going right but go forward, up and down over old earthworks for 100 yards on the edge of the escarpment. Again there are extensive views. Note below the brow of the hill a square stone block—Huddlestone's Table, where the King of Mercia said farewell to his guests who had been to the dedication of Winchcombe Abbey. Now bear right on a good path, away from the escarpment toward a golfers' sighting pole (an iron mast) 200 yards away among Iron Age earthworks. The path bears left, then forward for 600 yards with the escarpment on the left. The path climbs over Cleeve Cloud, the cliffs on the left being a mecca for rock climbers. Keep along the edge as the path descends slowly for 400 yards to where it divides. Take the upper path and again at the next fork in 50 yards. In 200 yards the view opens out and the car parks at Cleeve Hill can be seen. Keep to the path going towards the house and stables, then choose the one most suitable to reach your destination.

(6b) To return to Winchcombe

At the radio masts turn right along a broad track with a wall on the left for half a mile, passing a group of trees on the left. Soon there are extensive views over Cheltenham. At a second group of trees on the left, ignore a gate at a signboard and in 200 yards ignore the track going down at the end of the fence on the left. 30 yards from this you will reach two trees on the right, known as 'The Three Sisters'.

Now continue the walk from the paragraph marked (1) in the long route.

Shorter route from Prestbury and Cleeve Hill (6½ or 4 miles)

Follow the appropriate route to the end of the paragraph marked (3).

Turn half-right along this cross-track which soon brings a wall and trees on the left. After 600 yards the track bears left round trees and a valley goes off on the right (ignore all tracks on the right). You are now in a wild landscape, quite unfamiliar to many who go on Cleeve Hill, and reminiscent of mountain areas. The track leaves the trees and in a few yards divides. Take the left-hand track which in 200 yards bears right and descends to a pool of water known as the 'Washpool'. You will no doubt linger here a while.

Keep the pool on the left and follow the inflowing stream, after 100 yards crossing at a suitable point to bring the stream on the right. In a further 100 yards the stream ends at a spring. The path now ascends a narrow dry valley. In about 300 yards the valley divides; take the left-hand fork and soon the radio masts appear ahead. The path climbs gradually and in 400 yards a junction of paths is reached. Go straight ahead on a good path which climbs for 600 yards to meet a good cross-track with the radio masts 250 yards away on the right. Go to these.

Now go to paragraph (6) or (6a) in the long route as appropriate.

Shorter route from Winchcombe (6½ miles)

Follow the route via Belas Knap to the end of the paragraph marked (5).

From the gate go straight ahead on a good path. After 100 yards ignore the Cotswold Way new route sign and keep on forward. In 700 yards a cross-track is reached (radio masts on your left). Here turn half-right. The path now descends into a valley which gradually narrows and may seem desolate. Ignore all tracks left or right but keep going down the valley. In about three-quarters of a mile a spring will be reached, the stream flowing towards a pool which will soon be seen ahead. This is the 'Washpool'. 100 yards before reaching it cross the stream so that it is on the right. When you decide to continue, go ahead from the lower end of the pool on a good track, which bears left, climbing slightly. In 300 yards the track bears right round the end of a wood (ignore tracks on the left). In 600 yards an inclined track coming down on the left will be met and a sharp right turn must be made to go down this track.

Now continue the walk from the paragraph marked (4) in the long route.

Walk 4   **OVER LECKHAMPTON HILL TO**
THE CHURN VALLEY

Circular walk over Leckhampton Hill to Coberley and Cowley, returning via Upper Coberley, Seven Springs and Charlton Kings Common (8 or 5 miles).

1-inch map no. 144. 2½-inch map sheet SO 91. 1:50,000 map no. 163.

Local bus service from Cheltenham, no. 590 or 591 to the 'Foot of the hill', Leckhampton. Country bus service from Cheltenham to Swindon, no. 561 to Seven Springs (from the bus stop take the Gloucester road, A436, to reach, in about 300 yards, a lay-by on the right where the Seven Springs are located).

There are two small car parks in Daisy Bank Road, Leckhampton; the first off the road just on the right; the second 100 yards further along on the right-hand side of the road. There is a lay-by at Seven Springs on the Gloucester-Andoversford road (A436).

This circular route goes over Leckhampton Hill, passing the Devil's Chimney, along the Cotswold escarpment, then through Hartley Bottom to Coberley, continuing to Cowley and Cockleford. After climbing to Upper Coberley and descending to Seven Springs the walk continues over Charlton Kings Common, crossing the watershed twice en route. On a clear day the walk affords magnificent views over the surrounding countryside.

The walk may be shortened by starting at Seven Springs.

The starting point for the walk is the junction of Leckhampton Road and Old Bath Road, known locally as the **'Foot of the hill'**. It is not near the old part of Leckhampton or the church.

Go down Old Bath Road for 200 yards and turn right up Pilford Road to go over a stile at the end of the left-hand pavement. Climb the field bearing very slightly right so that there are scattered thorn bushes on the left. After 100 yards go along a well-defined path up the centre of the field. At the top bear right along a raised bank to go over a stile on the left at the field corner. In a few yards go over a second stile into Daisy Bank Road at the second car park. Cross the road, go over a stile and ascend the inclined track, an old tramway from the quarry above.

If parked in the first car park, take one of the paths on the left of the parking area, which leads to the inclined track, turn right and ascend.

At the top of the incline the path goes straight ahead and is signposted 'Devil's Chimney'. The path climbs steeply in three stages, the first is longest, the other two quite short, but there are less steep portions between which give excuse for breathtaking views across Cheltenham and Severn Vale to the Malvern Hills. Notice on the left the cliffs crumbling after winter frosts — geology in action. Water falling on this side of the hill flows to the river Severn.

Continue along the path to the **Devil's Chimney**, a column of rock on the right just below the edge of the cliff. On top of the cliff behind is an Iron Age camp. From the Devil's Chimney the path goes forward, rising a little as it bears slightly left, then bearing right along the grassy escarpment. If clear, on the right, views will be obtained of May Hill with its clump of trees, the Forest of Dean and the Black Mountains across the Severn Valley. Continue until a quarry is reached on the right, the path now descending to a narrow road at Salterley Grange. Now go to the paragraph marked (1).

An alternative easier route from the top of the incline is to turn half-right at the signpost along a path between trees, then almost immediately take the left fork at a junction, on to a narrow path with a wall on the right. Follow this path, having trees and an occasional house on the right. It passes below the Devil's Chimney (on the left) giving a more impressive view than from above. Eventually the path divides; ignore the descending path on the right but take the path climbing steadily, below cliffs, to come out on top of the escarpment. Turn right to reach a quarry and keeping this on the right go round the quarry to descend to a narrow road at **Salterley Grange.**

(1) Turn left up the road, ignore the track on the right at the top of the hill, and go past a house on the left to a junction. The left-hand track leads to another car park, so take the road half-right, heading for Hartley Farm about half a mile away. Almost at the farm buildings turn right along a farm track,

having a belt of trees and a wall on the left. Go through the third
gate on the left, turning half-right to descend into Hartley
Bottom. Rainfall in this valley drains to the river Thames, so you
have crossed the watershed.

In the valley bottom turn half-right (ignore the path rising up
to cottages on the left), go down a path passing a plantation and
then an old building on the right. Almost immediately go over a
stile into a field with a wood and wall on the left. Follow this wall
and where the wood ends there is a stile on the left leading into a
meadow. Go along parallel to the wood on the left past the
playing fields to a stile in the left-hand corner of the field. The
big pink house on the left is Seven Springs House, owned by
Gloucestershire County Council and used for school parties
studying the countryside. On going over the stile, keep along the
field side with hedge or fence on the left until a stile is reached at
the Gloucester-Andoversford road (A436). Be careful descending the bank on the roadside as this is a very busy road.

Cross and go left for 10 yards, then turn right at a signposted
bridle path. The path goes round a large field with a hedge on the
left. In 120 yards the path bears right and in another 250 yards it
enters a sunken lane where a path comes in on the right. The lane
leads into **Coberley**. Now go to the paragraph marked (2).

From Seven Springs

On leaving the lay-by turn right along the road towards
Gloucester for about 200 yards. Go through an iron kissing gate
on the left-hand side of the road, just below road level. Turn half-
right to go over the brow of the hill to a stile in the field corner. Go
over and continue in the same direction with a hedge on the left. In
250 yards the path enters a sunken lane where a path comes in on
the right. The lane leads into **Coberley**.

(2) On reaching the metalled road, go forward, passing on the
right a cross on the green; go over the next road and down a tarred
path between houses to come out on to another road. Immediately
opposite is a wooden kissing gate to which you will return if the
church is visited.

COBERLEY. The church and Coberley Court are about a quarter of
a mile along the road to the left. The church is entered through
a large archway on the right of the road, then round a garden to
the church porch. This and the tower are the oldest parts. In the
church are effigies of Sir Thomas Berkley and his wife, the
latter, from an earlier marriage, being the mother of Dick
Whittington.

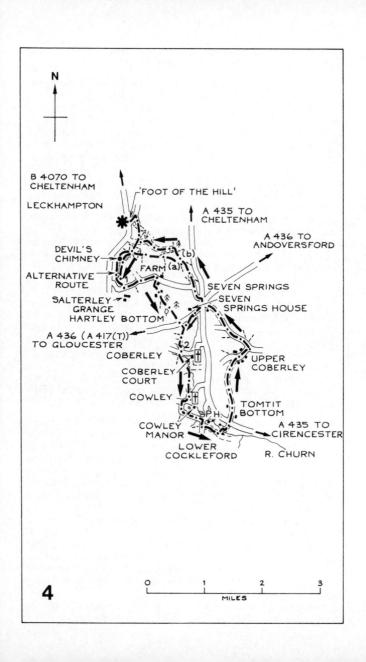

N

B 4070 TO
CHELTENHAM

LECKHAMPTON

'FOOT OF THE HILL'

A 435 TO
CHELTENHAM

A 436 TO
ANDOVERSFORD

DEVIL'S
CHIMNEY

(b)

FARM (a)

ALTERNATIVE
ROUTE

SEVEN SPRINGS

SEVEN
SPRINGS HOUSE

SALTERLEY
GRANGE
HARTLEY BOTTOM

A 436 (A 417(T))
TO GLOUCESTER

COBERLEY

UPPER
COBERLEY

COBERLEY
COURT

COWLEY

TOMTIT
BOTTOM

P H

A 435 TO
CIRENCESTER

COWLEY
MANOR

LOWER
COCKLEFORD

R. CHURN

4

0   1   2   3
MILES

On the left of the kissing gate note the spring and well which recently supplied water to the village.

To continue, pass through the kissing gate, down a short path, and over a stile and footbridge to turn half left across the field. Aim for an electricity pole midfield and keep the same direction to a stile near the field corner. Cross the lane diagonally right and go through a wooden gate into a field with a fence on the left. At the end of the fence go half-left across the field to bring trees on the right and in a few yards cross a wooden footbridge over a stream coming from the right. Go up the bank and turn right for 50 yards alongside the stream. Turn left at the first hedge, keeping this on the right for 250 yards until a gap in the hedge is reached. Pass through and look half-left for a wall corner some 500 yards ahead. Cross the field aiming for the wall corner (there will be a clump of trees on the right), negotiating an iron fence before reaching the wall. The path continues in the same direction, with a wall on the right, to a gate and stile leading into the road at **Cowley.** Bear slightly right along the road to the next corner.

COWLEY. On the left at the corner is the entrance to Cowley Manor and church. The manor is owned by Gloucestershire County Council and is used as a conference centre and for other activities. It is not open to the public. The house was built in 1674 and enlarged about a hundred years ago for Sir James Horlick who built most of the houses in the village. The grounds contain terraces and lakes which will be seen later on the walk.

The church in the manor grounds dates from 1200 but was restored in the late nineteenth century. It contains a stone pulpit and a reredos made of mosaics and marble.

Go forward from the manor entrance and along the first road on the left. As you go along this road there are good views of the south facade of the manor and the ornamental grounds. Further along, the land on either side is used for youth activities. After half a mile the road leads to a T junction and facing it is the Green Dragon Inn. (If you feel energetic, turn left and 200 yards down the road on the left, is the lowest of the manor lakes. Return to the T junction.)

At this junction turn right up the road and take the first lane on the left leading to **Lower Cockleford.** In about 600 yards where the lane turns right, with a house facing the lane, there is a signposted footpath on the left. This leads down to a footbridge over the river Churn, a tributary of the Thames. Cross and go up the drive of the Mill House (with daffodils on both sides in spring) to reach the Cheltenham-Cirencester road (A435).

Cross this busy road carefully and ascend the road opposite. On the left is Tomtit's Bottom. The road soon becomes a track which is followed for a mile to the hamlet of Upper Coberley. As you walk, look across the valley on the left for views of Cowley and Coberley with Shab Hill behind, complete with radio masts. The hills forming this skyline are the watershed. (Ignore all tracks on the right.) The track leads to the road at **Upper Coberley** where turn right. Follow this road for 500 yards to a T junction, turning left. Note the various barns, all similar, with roofs supported on stone columns. In 200 yards, as the road bears left, ignore the bridle road to Wistley Hill. Continue on the metalled road for 400 yards to pass New Farm on the left as the road bears right. In 300 yards at the next junction fork right on a farm track. This gradually descends and in half a mile reaches the junction of the A435 and A436 roads at **Seven Springs**. Cross the A435 road.

If a visit is to be made to the Seven Springs or if the walk started there turn left and then right along the Gloucester road for about 300 yards to the lay-by, the springs being on the left in a hollow. Many regard these springs as the true source of the Thames since they are further from London than Thames Head spring (the official source) and never run dry.

To continue the walk, return to the cross-roads and turn left towards Cheltenham. After 80 yards, a minor road starts on the left deviating slowly from the main road. This is part of the Cotswold Way and once again you are in the Severn drainage area. Follow this road until it turns left. Go forward along a track which soon enters a wood, continuing for 600 yards until the wood on the left ends. There are now two possibilities: (a) a climb on to Charlton Kings Common escarpment rewarded by good views; (b) little climbing but with more restricted views.

(a) On emerging from the wood, a narrow path will be seen climbing the steep hillside. This leads to a path along the edge of the escarpment with a broad track below and Wistley Hill across the valley on the right. The path slowly bears left and in 600 yards becomes a broad path where a path comes up on the right. The path keeps to the edge of the escarpment overlooking Charlton Kings and Cheltenham, with views across to Cleeve Hill, Bredon and the Malvern Hills. Keep to the main path, ignoring others for about half a mile. Where the broad path bears left appearing to leave the edge, take the narrower path almost straight ahead. The path descends with the brow of the hill on the left and bushes on the right, and later giving a view of the incline up which you walked near the start of the walk. The path joins a rough track; turn right down this to reach the top of the incline. You have now completed the circuit. Go down the incline to Daisy Bank Road and the car parks. To the bus route, go over two stiles and descend the field to Pilford Road and Old Bath Road.

(b) On emerging from the wood, continue forward on a good

track until reaching a wood on the right. In 100 yards there is a junction of paths. Take the path going off at 'ten o' clock' to the direction in which you have come. It climbs a little for 100 yards then houses will be seen ahead. The path now drops and continues towards a hedge on the right. In about a quarter of a mile it joins a gravelly track by some electricity cables. This is the beginning of Daisy Bank Road which becomes metalled a quarter of a mile further along. This leads directly to the car park at the foot of the incline and you have completed the circuit. Continue along the road for the other car park. To reach the bus route, turn right at the foot of the incline, going over two stiles and following the path down the field to Pilford Road and Old Bath Road.

Walk 5   AROUND THE ROMAN COLN VALLEY

Circular walk from Hangman's Stone to Chedworth returning via the Roman villa and Yanworth (9 or 2 miles).

1-inch map no. 144. 2½-inch map sheet no. SP 01. 1:50,000 map no. 163.

Park at Hangman's Stone on the London road (A40) (grid reference 089151), 1¾ miles west of Northleach. Car park at the Roman villa.

There is no bus service.

The walk starts at a lay-by on the A40 at **Hangman's Stone** at the junction with the road to Fossebridge and Cirencester. It goes by field tracks to Stowell church, through the park to Fossebridge, then to Chedworth village. The return is made via Chedworth woods to the Roman villa and the village of Yanworth.

A short circular walk from Chedworth to the Roman villa (or vice versa) is also described.

From the lay-by go along the minor road (signposted to Fossebridge and Cirencester, and part of the Salt Way) for 300 yards, then turn right along a lane (signposted 'Oxpens Farm') for 200 yards to **Oxpens**. The lane goes between buildings, then bears left uphill to a Y junction. Take the right-hand fork passing a house and along a path with a wood on the right. In 300 yards, at the end of the field, the path goes through a gateway and becomes a good track for about half a mile, keeping to the side of a wood and finally bearing left to meet a road (from Northleach to Chedworth).

To visit **Stowell** church cross the road and go along a metalled drive for 400 yards (marked strictly private and no through road), then turn right and shortly left, the church being on the left.

STOWELL PARK AND CHURCH. The mansion adjacent to the church was built in Elizabethan times but has been modified and enlarged since. From it there are magnificent views over the park and the Coln Valley.

The church is well maintained, part Norman, with an old font. It contains one of the best examples of a Doom painting. The biggest surviving portion shows Mary and the Apostles watching the separation of souls into the saved and the lost. The pews are modern, beautifully made by the estate carpenter.

To continue the walk return to the Chedworth road. Turn down the road for a quarter of a mile, turning left along the road signposted to Fossebridge and Chedworth. Where this road turns right, go through a wooden gate with a house on the left. The path is a few yards to the left of a stream and crosses a meadow, gradually approaching a wall on the left. Go through a gate in this wall 80 yards from the field corner. Go alongside the wall on the right to pass through a gate ahead (neglect the gate on the right) into a field with a fence and wood on the right. Go to a gate near the field corner (ignoring two gates on the right into the wood). Through the gate turn almost right, crossing the field diagonally (this may be ploughed) to the corner of a plantation ahead. Continue in the same direction to a gateway in the top corner of the field. Bear right to go along the side of the field with a wood on the right, continuing on a concrete track. Where a cross-track is met go ahead on a path (with a concrete base) through conifers. (This area once contained a number of temporary buildings.) In 250 yards the path bears right, coming to a big concrete slab. Make for the far right-hand corner of the slab and turn right down a concrete path for 20 yards then continue forward and bear left for 50 yards (the last few yards may be overgrown) to a gate into a field. Go down the field, approaching slowly the wall on the 'left to reach a track at the bottom, leaving by a gate on to the Fosse Way (A429, and part of the Roman road from Bath to Lincoln). Go down the road, over the river Coln (a tributary of the Thames), passing the **Fossebridge Hotel** on the right.

Go up the hill, in 150 yards passing a road on the right. Just beyond the road, a footpath starts at a gate on the right, immediately above a house. Keep to the right-hand field boundary. After 150 yards the path turns left, with the hedge on the right. At the field corner go through a gate, keeping ahead so that a wall is on the left and a stream on the right. In 300 yards go over a stile with a wall on the left and alongside the stream. Soon there is a wood up on the left and then a pond on the right. Continue along the valley, finally with a wall on the right, and going through a gate on to the road at a corner. Turn right for 100 yards to a junction at **Pancakehill**. Turn left up a lane, passing a lane on the right in 170 yards. In a further 100 yards the road turns left and then in another 100 yards turns right. Take the track ahead to the right of the entrance to Green Hill Farm. In 250 yards the track bends left and continues for three-quarters of a mile (ignore all cross-tracks) giving views across the valley of **Chedworth** and coming out on to a road. Turn left, following the winding road into the valley and up into the village. On the left is the Seven Tuns inn where liquid refreshment may be obtained.

CHEDWORTH. At the top of the village street, in the inn garden on the right, is an old water wheel. Turn right to go to the church. The most outstanding feature of the church is the Norman arch between the nave and the tower. The splendid carved pulpit is fifteenth-century. It is interesting to see that the stone mason used Arabic numerals to inscribe the date 1485 on the lower face of the turret.

From the church go back to the road, turning left, the road soon bearing right. Ignore the road going down on the right but go ahead along the road signposted 'Footpath to Roman Villa'. At the end of the road go over a stile and follow the path, keeping to the left side of the field. This leads to a stile into a field. Aim for the far corner of the field and go over a stile. Go forward 50 yards to a path going up on the left to a stile with a wood on the left. Turn right for 10 yards to go through a hunting gate in the field corner and alongside the wall on the right. Go over a stile by the wall, across a narrow field with a fence on the left to another stile. The path now goes to a gate into a wood and in 50 yards reaches a stile. The path is well defined and goes through Chedworth Woods for 600 yards before dropping to a junction of paths. Turn right down a path signposted 'Roman Villa', passing under the disused railway, to arrive at the **Roman Villa** on the left.

CHEDWORTH ROMAN VILLA. This was discovered in 1864 and is National Trust property. There are tessellated pavements, hypocausts and baths, all roofed over, and a small museum. In the garden there is a Nymphaeum — an octagonal basin filled by a spring. The villa is open to the public at certain times.

At the villa exit, turn left down the road for 400 yards to crossroads. Here turn right through green gates along a good track for one and a quarter miles. Chedworth Woods are on the right and the river Coln on the left. The track ends at the corner of a road, where turn left, crossing the river (with an old mill on the left). The road bends left up the hill. As you climb, the mansion in Stowell Park may be seen on the hill over on the right. In about 500 yards as the road bears left, a gate will be found on the right. Go through and cross the field to the upper far corner by aiming at a wall corner and then keeping the wall on the left. A gate gives access to a lane. Go along it and turn

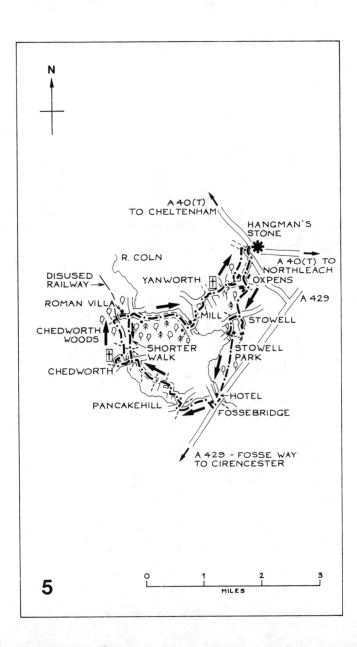

N

A 40(T)
TO CHELTENHAM

HANGMAN'S
STONE

R. COLN

DISUSED
RAILWAY →

YANWORTH

A 40(T) TO
NORTHLEACH
OXPENS

A 429

ROMAN VILLA

MILL

CHEDWORTH
WOODS

STOWELL

SHORTER
WALK

STOWELL
PARK

CHEDWORTH

HOTEL

PANCAKEHILL

FOSSEBRIDGE

A 429 - FOSSE WAY
TO CIRENCESTER

0   1   2   3
MILES

5

right at the road through the village of **Yanworth**. Where the road turns right, turn left for a few yards, then right down a metalled lane to the church on the left.

YANWORTH. The church is late twelfth-century with a Norman window in the north wall of the north transept. The font is Norman and the east window is old glass.

From the church turn left going between buildings and turning left for a few yards, then right to a T junction. Turn left for 20 yards, then right down a metalled lane. Follow the road some 500 yards into a valley and up and, where a wood touches the road on the right, turn left over a stile by a gate. Follow along the left wall of the field for about 150 yards to a gate in the far corner. Go through and turn left along a field, with another wall on your left, to a five-bar gate ahead. Go through the gate and turn right up the slight rise. The path continues for some 700 yards, passing under overhead cables, to reach a farm track. Turn right for 100 yards to the minor road down which you started the walk. A left turn leads to the lay-by on the main road (A40).

A shorter walk from Chedworth

Follow the route described from Chedworth to the Roman villa.

At the villa exit turn left down the road for 250 yards. Turn right up a green track, signposted 'Bridle path to Chedworth'. In 50 yards ignore the track on the right. In another 150 yards ignore the track on the left. Keep up the main track climbing steadily. In 100 yards, at a Y junction, take the left track. In 100 yards this becomes a sunken track, inclined to be muddy for a short distance. If muddy, take to the right bank just above the track. Again you are in Chedworth Woods and you may find the foot-prints of deer. In a further 200 yards go over a cross-track and continue up, bearing left for 50 yards to a gate. The path now winds up for 150 yards with a wall on the left and goes through a gate. (Ignore the cross-track into a field just before reaching the gate.) Go up a short track out of the wood into a field with a wall on the left. Keep to the wall for 200 yards to go through a large iron gate. Keep alongside the wall or fence on the right. The path descends, giving views of Chedworth across the valley, to a farm track and road junction. Cross the track and turn down the road into the valley and up into the village.

Walk 6   **PAINSWICK TO BISLEY**

Circular walk from Painswick through Slad to Bisley, returning via Bulls Cross (10, 7½, or 4 miles).

1-inch map no. 156. 2½-inch map sheet no. SO 80. 1:50,000 map nos. 162 and 163.

Buses from Cheltenham, Gloucester and Stroud.

Car parking in Painswick.

The walk descends to the Painswick Stream, climbs Juniper Hill, descends into the Slad valley, then over Swift's Hill, round Lypiatt Park into the Toadsmoor Valley and along this to Bisley. The return is made via Sydenham's Farm, Down Hill, crossing the Slad valley, up to Bulls Cross, then descending to and alongside the Painswick Stream and back to Painswick.

Shorter routes from Painswick and Bisley are also described.

The walks are hilly, the long route involving a total climb in the region of 2000 feet, the short route from Painswick 700 feet, and that from Bisley 1300 feet.

PAINSWICK. The church is approached through a picturesque lychgate built in 1901 from old timber from the belfry. The churchyard is famous for its clipped yews. The church probably dates from the fourteenth century. Near the rear exit from the churchyard are the old iron stocks.

In the village are many sixteenth-century buildings and it is worthwhile walking about the narrow streets. The post office is a timber-framed building with an old insurance mark on a gable.

From the car park turn left down Stamages Lane and in a quarter of a mile, at the crossroads, go ahead down Stepping Stone Lane, crossing the stream and going up the hill for 60 yards. Turn right along a track signposted 'To the Sheephouse'. In 700 yards the house is reached. It is a typical seventeenth-century Cotswold house, with dovecotes in the gables. At the house turn left over a car park and lawn to an iron squeezer stile between two wooden gates. Continue up the hill between a fence on the right and a hedge to a second stile. This path may be rather overgrown. Continue upwards with a hedge on the left for 150 yards, then go through a stile into a field keeping to the right-hand boundary and coming out through a wooden gate on to a metalled lane.

Turn left for 50 yards, then right at a T junction signposted to Bulls Cross and Sheepscombe. In 15 yards turn right along a stony track. After 100 yards, where the track bears right, ignore the track going half-left. The track climbs steadily, giving extensive views across the valley to Edge, Pitchcombe and Whiteshill. The track leads over the hill and across a field, bringing a wall on the right. At the field boundary go ahead for 10 yards to the point where the routes diverge **(1)**.

(1) Turn right through a gate and along a farm track marked Worgans Farm. The track goes between farm buildings and past the farm on the right. 50 yards beyond the farm turn left through a gateway into a field, keeping to the hedge on the left. At the lower field corner turn left into a wood for 20 yards to a gate on the right and into a field. Keep to the side of the wood on the left. In 250 yards pass through a line of trees and continue down the field with trees on the left. In 150 yards go through a gate into a lane with a house on the right. In 200 yards the lane bends left, but take a metalled path on the right leading down to the Birdlip-Stroud road (B4070). Be careful at the road as the path is steep and there is no pavement along the roadside. Cross the road and turn right for about 100 yards. (To the left is the village of **Slad.**)

SLAD.The village straggles for half a mile along the Birdlip-Stroud road. This is the country of Laurie Lee, who in his book *Cider with Rosie* described life in the village half a century ago.

Opposite the lower exit from Woodside House, next to the Star Inn, take a narrow obscure path between the wall of the road and a low building, descending for 20 yards to a stile, where turn left to reach a metalled lane by a house. Go half-left along the lane in front of the house. (Should you miss the obscure path, turn left down the lane just beyond the inn, in 50 yards passing a house on the left.) The lane winds uphill to a junction. Turn left and in a few yards turn right along the lane. In 200 yards pass between Knapp House on the right and farm buildings on the left. In 100 yards, where the lane bears left, go forward up a visible path to the top of **Swift's Hill**, giving extensive views over Slad and Stroud. Continue on the path in the same general direction, bringing a wall and fence on the left and a deep valley on the right. The path descends a little and enters a wood near the head of the valley. Bear right to a stile in a fence and over this bear right to go over another stile. Now turn left between bushes for 20 yards into a field. Turn right, keeping some 15 yards above the right-hand hedge, crossing a small dip to a gap in the hedge ahead leading to the next field. Keep to the hedge on the left, then cross to a stile over a barbed-wire fence. Turn left over a fence and alongside a fence on the left, then over the fence ahead. Turn right to go through a small gate on to a path to Fennell's Farm on the right of a track. Go along the track, which bears left with buildings on the left and in a further 150 yards leads to a minor road at Lypiatt Lodge. Turn right and then left along the road signposted to Middle and Nether Lypiatt. **Lypiatt Park** is on the left.

LYPIATT PARK. The house dates from the fourteenth century but it was modified in the nineteenth century when the embattled parapets were added. The stables, built to resemble a castle, are of this date. In the grounds is a fourteenth-century dovecote. It is said that Guy Fawkes and the gunpowder plotters met at Lypiatt Park. There is no public access to the house or park.

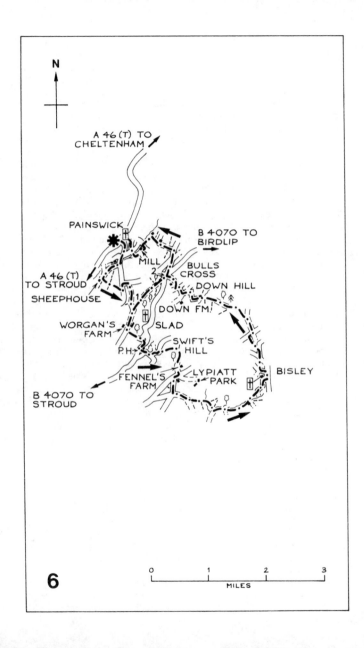

N

A 46 (T) TO
CHELTENHAM

PAINSWICK

B 4070 TO
BIRDLIP

MILL

BULLS
CROSS

A 46 (T)
TO STROUD

DOWN HILL

SHEEPHOUSE

DOWN FM.

1

WORGAN'S
FARM

SLAD

P.H.

SWIFT'S
HILL

LYPIATT
PARK

BISLEY

FENNEL'S
FARM

B 4070 TO
STROUD

6

0   1   2   3

MILES

At the first road junction turn left on a lane signposted to Ferris Court and Home Farm. After 500 yards, where the road bears right, there is an entry on the left into fields. Go through an iron gate (the right-hand one of two), keeping near the wall on the left. Cross the field (with views of Lypiatt House on the left), then go over a barbed-wire fence (using a fallen tree as a stile) at the field corner. Go ahead down the next field, with a fence on the left and over a stile in the field corner. The path, near the wall on the left, descends steeply through a wood. At the bottom cross a stream by means of an old bridge and go up the field ahead with a wall on the left. Go over a stile a few yards to the right of the corner and into a wood. Go forward 20 yards, then turn right along a good path through the wood. In 250 yards the path descends to a house at a cross-track. Turn left along the track, in a few yards passing a building on the right. The track now becomes a path along the bottom of a wood with a wall or fence on the right. After 350 yards cross the remains of a wall stile by the fence on the right. The path continues by the fence to reach a stone stile into a lane. Turn left up the lane (ignore the stone stile on the right), and in 40 yards take a path on the right almost opposite a house on the left. The path goes through a wood with a stream in the bottom on the right. At the end of the wood go over a stile into a field and along the valley by the stream on the right. The path undulates but is fairly well defined. In 500 yards go over a stile by a house on the right. In 100 yards go over a stile, crossing the stream and keeping near the left-hand field boundary to a small gate in the corner. Bear left through the gate and up a green track to go out through a gate into a lane. Turn left up the lane to a junction. This is **Bisley.** Ignore the road on the right but go up to the next junction. Turn right and in 20 yards steps on the left lead up to the church and the Bear Inn. On going forward along the road the seven wells are passed on the left. The road goes forward, then bears left passing the church lychgate up on the left and going on to the Stirrup Cup, also on the left. A left turn before the inn takes one to the church and Bear Inn. Refreshment may be obtained at both the inns.

BISLEY. The church is fourteenth-century, restored in the nineteenth century. In the churchyard is a thirteenth-century poor souls' light, said to have been built over a well, down which a priest fell to his death one night. It was used for candles for masses for the poor to be said and is believed to be the only one in England outside a church. Below the church are seven wells which are decorated with flowers on Ascension Day. The Bear Inn is the old court-house, the columns supporting the upper storey dating from the seventeenth century. On the left, some 25 yards in front of the Bear Inn, is the village lock-up, dated 1824.

From the church go to the Bear Inn. Here turn left along the road for 20 yards, then turn half-right through a stile by the car park. Cross the field diagonally to a stile. The path leads through new development to a cul-de-sac which goes to a T junction. Turn right for 25 yards, then left for 30 yards to a Y junction. Take the right fork, signposted 'The Camp and Birdlip'. In 100 yards, opposite a house, take the path half-left between walls. This may be rather overgrown. The path leads into a field. Keep to the hedge and wall on the left to a gate in the field corner. Through the gate keep to the wall on the right, passing a house on the right, and ahead to go through a gate on to a road. Cross and go ahead on a road signposted to Sydenham's and The Scrubs, and in a quarter of a mile passing a triangulation point in a field on the right. In 100 yards, where the road bears right, go over a stile on the left into a field. Keep to the wall on the left, going down the field, through a gate and down the next field to a small gate ahead on to a green track (ignore the gate and path on the right leading towards a farm). Go down this to a Y junction. Take the left fork on a path winding steeply down the side of a wood, with a valley on the left. Near the bottom of the valley pass a house on the left, the path leading into a lane. Go ahead, passing a house on the right. In about 200 yards, by two garages, leave the lane. Go along the path ahead for 10 yards then take the path on the left (not forward in front of the house). In a few yards the path turns right below the house mentioned above (ignore the path on the left). The path now climbs slightly to a cross path with a house on the right. Turn left, again with the valley on the left. In 100 yards pass a house on the right, and in a further 100 yards at a Y junction, fork left down a path which in 100 yards leads through a small gate. Go down the field, keeping to the wall or hedge on the right, to a stile in the field corner.

Over the stile cross a stream by a bridge and turn half-left up a track to a farm and house. The track bears right by the house and joins a metalled lane. Go along this lane which soon bears right, passing a house on the right and climbing steadily, then bearing left to join a road. Go ahead down the road for 100 yards to where this bears left. Here turn right on a track to Trillgate. After 200 yards, at a Y junction, take the track going down left. In another 120 yards go through an iron gate on the right of the track and down a field with a fence on the left. At the bottom of the field go over a bridge, through a gate and up the field, with a hedge on the left, to go over a stile to the right of farm buildings (Trillgate Farm) on to a metalled lane. Turn right along the lane which climbs and winds up to **Bulls Cross** on the B4070 **(2).**

(2) Take the road signposted 'Sheepscombe'. After a quarter of a mile take a track on the left, opposite houses, to Dell Farm. Go down the track and bear right into the farmyard, with a

house on the right. Through the farmyard go to the left of the
Dutch barn towards a bungalow on the right. (Behind this is a
Friends' burial ground dated 1658). Before reaching the bunga-
low cross half-left over a farm track.

Over the farm track cross rough ground to reach a path seen
half-left, with a wall and fence on the left, to a wooden gate in
the left-hand field corner. Through the gate go down the
left-hand side of the field to a wooden stile on the left in the
corner, giving access to a field with a wall on the right. (Over the
wall is an old mill, now a house known as Lovedays.) Keep to the
wall, then go over a stile on the right just before the next field
boundary. Go down to the riverbank, over a stile and along the
riverside, emerging through a gate on to a road. Cross, bearing
left, and go along a metalled track on the right of the road,
signposted 'Brooklands Close'. On the right is the river and old
pin mills. At the house go ahead along the lawn, with the house
on the right, and along a path between a wall and a hedge to go
over a stile into a field. Keep to the hedge on the right, then go
over a second stile. Continue alongside the hedge on the left.
Soon the path is between hedges and bears right down to a lane.
Turn right for a short distance, then left to a metalled lane. On
the left is Painswick Mill, originally a cloth and later a pin mill,
now a house, the gardens of which are sometimes open to the
public. At a T junction cross the road and go up a path ahead
leading to a road. 250 yards up the road look on the left for a
narrow metalled path which soon becomes a lane, giving a view
of the church ahead. The lane leads to a small car park with an
entrance to the churchyard in the left-hand corner. Go through
the churchyard and turn left down the main road to the car park
from which the walk started.

Shorter route from Painswick (4 miles)

Follow the long route to the end of the paragraph marked (1).

Turn left, over a stile by a gate, into a field keeping alongside
the wall on the left to a stile ahead. The path goes forward by the
wall with a wood on the right. In 300 yards the path becomes a
broad track. Keep straight ahead, ignoring entries into fields on
the left. Soon the wood on the right thins out but keep along the
main track for 500 yards, at which point it enters a wood and soon
starts to descend. Ignore side tracks and in 400 yards the track
leads to the Birdlip-Stroud road (B4070) at Bulls Cross.

Now go to the paragraph marked (2) in the long route.

Shorter route from Bisley (7½ miles)

Follow the long route from Bisley to the end of the paragraph
marked (2).

Cross the road and take a broad track half-left towards a wood.

At a Y junction at the start of the wood, go ahead on a track with a wall on the right. In 100 yards, at a Y junction, keep ahead climbing steadily and keeping to the main track. In about 250 yards the track enters a clearing and there are fields on the right. Go ahead on a good track, ignoring entries into the fields. In 500 yards, the track becomes a path on the edge of the wood, with a wall on the right. In 300 yards, at the end of the wood, go over a stile and across a field alongside the wall on the right to a stile by a gate. Cross a track and go ahead along a track marked 'Worgans Farm'. Now continue the walk from the paragraph marked (1) in the long route.

Walk 7   OVER THE HILLS ROUND DURSLEY

Circular walk from Dursley over Cam Long Down and Uley Bury to Uley, returning via Whiteway Hill to Dursley (8 or 6 miles). 1-inch map no. 156. 2½-inch map sheet no. ST 79. 1:50,000 map no. 162.
Buses from Bristol, Cheltenham, Gloucester and Stroud.
Car parking in Dursley.

The walk starts from the centre of Dursley and follows the Cotswold Way over Peaked Down and Cam Long Down to the Iron Age camp on Uley Bury, then descends to Uley village. The walk continues through Elcombe, over Whiteway Hill into the woods above Waterley Bottom and over the hill through Hermitage Wood to Dursley.

The walk may be shortened by using a more direct route from Uley to Dursley.

The walk affords magnificent views but the long route involves a total climb of some 1500 feet, the short route 900 feet.

DURSLEY is a busy small town with well-known engineering works. The Market House surmounted by a belfry is eighteenth-century, with the upper storeys supported on stone columns.
The church dates from the fourteenth century and is noted for its east window. It has a canopied triple sedilia and the bowl of the font is fourteenth-century.

From the Market House go down Long Street. At the end bear half-right up a lane (marked 'Private drive') for 50 yards, then turn left through a kissing gate.* Go up a steep path between hedges to another kissing gate and into a field. Cross this, going slightly right to a gate in the corner by the right-hand boundary,

---

* This path may be overgrown. Should it be impassable use the following alternative. At the end of Long Street turn left along the road and in 50 yards this bends right. In a further 50 yards turn right for 200 yards, then left. Continue up the road for half a mile, passing houses on the right, to a T junction with a road signposted 'Uley'. Now continue as follows.

with buildings on the left. Go through the gate ahead and keep alongside the fence on the left for 200 yards, then go over a stile on the left in the field corner and ahead on a path leading to a road. Turn right along the road for 400 yards, past houses on the right, to a T junction with a road signposted 'Uley'.

At this junction go half-right over a stile in a hedge and diagonally across the field, aiming between a house and barns, to go through a gate on to a road. Turn right for 40 yards and where the road bends left go through a hunting gate on the right, signposted 'Long Down', the path leading to the summit of Peaked Down (600 feet). There are now extensive views; eastwards to Uley Bury and Downham Hill; south to the woods on Breakheart Hill with the Tyndale Monument on Nibley Knoll; westwards across the Vale of Severn to the Forest of Dean and the Black Mountains; northwards up the Severn valley towards Stonehouse and Gloucester.

From the summit go forward and down towards a saddle. In 40 yards, at a junction of paths, bear slightly right down to the saddle. Here there are two paths climbing Cam Long Down — the left-hand one climbs steeply, the right-hand path less so, but keep to the main path. Both paths lead on to the summit of Cam Long Down (700 feet). Bear right along the ridge following a narrow path. At present the path leads down to a locked hunting gate but the right of way is over a stile about 100 yards to the right of the gate. Note the road in the valley below to which you are going. Go over the stile bearing slightly left across the field to a gap in the hedge ahead. Cross the field below, bearing slightly left to a stile some 20 yards to the right of a field corner, then go round the left-hand field boundary to a gate on to the road noted above. Go ahead along the road and where this turns right, turn left along a track, then right to pass through Hodgecombe Farm. Continue ahead and in 100 yards the track bears left, climbing steeply through a wood for 400 yards and emerging on to the Stroud-Dursley road (B4066). If the path through the wood is muddy, after a short distance use the bank on the left.

HETTY PEGLER'S TUMP.   This is a long barrow, 120 feet long, containing three burial chambers which yielded fifteen skeletons when excavated in 1854. It lies on the left of the B4066 road about half a mile away along the road to the left and can be entered by obtaining the key at Crawley Hill Cafe, about 250 yards along the road to the left.

To continue the walk, at the road turn right immediately leaving the road to go along an inclined track for 100 yards to a hunting gate and cattle grid on the right. Through the gate go along a

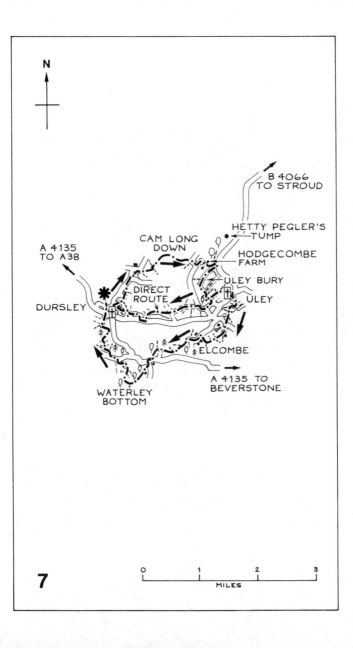

N

B 4066
TO STROUD

HETTY PEGLER'S
TUMP

CAM LONG
DOWN

HODGECOMBE
FARM

A 4135
TO A38

ULEY BURY

DIRECT
ROUTE

ULEY

DURSLEY

ELCOMBE

A 4135 TO
BEVERSTONE

WATERLEY
BOTTOM

7

0   1   2   3
MILES

broad path on the edge of **Uley Bury** (700 feet), eventually giving extensive views south and west. Turn left along the south-west edge of the Bury giving views over Uley.

ULEY BURY. This is an Iron Age hillfort enclosing a 32-acre site and dated about 200 B.C. It is surrounded by a single bank, ditch and counterscarp.

Just beyond another hunting gate and cattle grid turn right down a narrow path leading to a wood, ignoring paths on the right. Go down through the wood, over a stile with a wall on the right and down the side of the field to the left of cottages. Here turn left on a path signposted 'The Church'. Cross the field, keeping to the fence on the right, to go over a stile on to a path between fences. At a stile ahead into a field turn right through a gate on to a path between fences. Continue with houses on the right, to go over a stile and along a path between hedges, then alongside the churchyard into the road at **Uley.**

ULEY. The church is nineteenth-century but there has been a church on the site since the twelfth century. The interior is rather unusual. The reredos is of stone and marble.

From the church go down the main road and down the first road on the left (Woodstock Terrace). The road ends at a playing field, where turn right for 20 yards then left round the field to a road. Turn right and where the road turns right, bear slightly left to go over a stile into a field, with a stream some 50 yards to the left. Go straight ahead for 150 yards parallel to the power line on the left, then turn left between two poles to cross a stile and a footbridge. Continue in the same direction, going between a line of trees, aiming for the fourth tree on the right and crossing the field to a road at a gate opposite a farm drive. Cross the road and go up the drive towards Lye Farm with its interesting buildings. Just before the farm is reached go over the fence on the right to enter the next field and go anticlockwise round a prominent tree some 40 yards away, continuing to a gate in the far corner, with a lake 250 yards to the right. Beyond the lake is Shadwell, a school. Through the gate turn half-left, passing just to the left of a small knoll to a gateway into a field with a hedge on the right. Keep to the hedge to go over a bar stile, where turn right alongside the hedge to a stile by a gate, and along a track coming out to the right of houses, on to a lane at **Elcombe.** Turn left along the lane, which after 200 yards bears right. In a further 200 yards the lane bears left. Ignore the track going left in front of houses but go forward for a short distance to turn left, near a cattle grid, up a path between hedges passing a house on the left. The path becomes a sunken track between high banks and after 250 yards reaches a junction of tracks. Go straight ahead climbing steadily through a wood to reach, in some 400 yards, a cross-track and small clearing. This track is within 30 yards of the Dursley-Beverstone road (A4135), and a rather unusual house can be seen through the trees.

Turn right at the clearing and in 20 yards bear left at a Y junction. In about 400 yards a Y junction is reached. Take the left fork and in 100 yards the path leads to a junction of tracks. Turn left into a clearing and in 20 yards turn right along a path through the wood. Ignore side paths and in 200 yards emerge on to the A4135 road.

Turn right along the road and in 200 yards turn left along a minor road (with a house on the left) in front of a double-bend sign. In 150 yards (just before the road becomes steep) take a track half-right, descending steadily through a wood (ignore a track on the right). In about 150 yards ignore a track going up half-right and in a further 150 yards, just above a cottage on the left, bear right along a track which continues just within the wood, with fields on the left and giving glimpses into Waterley Bottom. The track winds through the wood and in about half a mile at a Y junction take the right fork climbing slowly to reach a track coming in on the right. Continue forward, and forward again at the next junction. Here there is a good view across the valley to the Tyndale Monument on Nibley Knoll. In about 150 yards a track comes in on the left but bear right for 120 yards to reach a minor road.

Turn left along the road for about 200 yards to an opening in the wood on the right. Here there is a path half-right along which you should go. To reach it, turn right for 10 yards then left through a gap in the wall and across to the path you require. The path is narrow but opens out later. Continue for some 500 yards, ignoring side paths, to a T junction where turn right, downhill. Ignore side paths and in 300 yards the path bears left to a cross-track. Cross to a path in the wood, contouring round the hill, first bearing right then left. After 700 yards a cross-track in a gully will be reached, going down on the right, but go forward on a path above houses (ignore paths on the left) to another junction, where turn right down to a metalled road which leads to the main road. Turn left and in 150 yards the starting point of the walk will be reached.

Direct route from Uley to Dursley

Retrace part of the route into Uley by taking the path on the top side of the church signposted 'Uley Bury and Whitecourt'. Follow the path over a stile by houses, ignoring an entry on the left. Go along the side of a field with houses and fence on the left. Pass through a gate and go on a path between fences bearing right to a gate, where turn left, between fences, to go over a stile into a field. Keep to the hedge on the left and go out through an iron gate on to a track with houses on the right. This shortly reaches a road. Go forward along the road to a junction with a chapel on the left. Bear right along the road signposted 'Coaley'. The road turns right by Angeston Nurseries. 20 yards beyond the corner turn left along a track with a wall on the left.

Continue along the track, passing a barn and a house on the right. 120 yards beyond, the track bears left by a house on the left. The track is now between hedges and can be muddy. In about 400 yards, where the track bears right to join a cross-track, go through a gate diagonally left across this track (there is a small footpath sign at the right-hand side of the gate). Cross the field, with a house on the left, to go through a gate. Cross the next field, aiming just to the left of a creeper-covered barn, and ignoring the path going half-right towards a farm, to reach another gate. Through this turn half-right to cross a fence some 25 yards away near the creeper-covered barn, but watch for a grass-concealed stream in a concrete channel a few feet in front of the fence. The fence is rather difficult to negotiate and the ground on the far side uneven and overgrown. In about 10 feet cross a stile beside the barn. Keep alongside the wall on the right, then cross the field to go through a wooden gate near the right-hand boundary into a field with a hedge on the left. After 200 yards the path bears right to cross a stream and immediately turns left to an iron gate. Cross the next field to a wooden gate ahead leading to a short track over the river Ewelme. Turn left and go through a farmyard to reach the Dursley-Stroud road (B4066), where turn right in front of Mawdsley's engineering works.

In about 300 yards, at a car park on the right, turn right on a path between fences round the outside of the car park. The path leads to and alongside the river. In about 300 yards the path passes a building on the left and leads to a metalled lane. Turn right for 20 yards, then left to a T junction. Turn right for 10 yards to take a footpath on the left (ignore the footpath ahead). This bears left, then becomes a track which crosses the river and continues as a road between the works buildings of Messrs R. A. Lister. Continue on the road and as it bears right notice a building on the left dated 1867, the original foundry of Sir Ashton Lister. Ignore Water Street on the left but turn left at the next junction. In a few yards turn left up Long Street to the town centre of **Dursley.**

Walk 8   **THROUGH PARKLAND SOUTH OF TETBURY**

Circular walk from Tetbury through Shipton Moyne to Easton Grey returning via Westonbirt (11, 7½, or 5 miles).
1-inch map no. 156. 2½-inch map sheet nos. ST 89, ST 88.

1:50,000 map nos. 162 and 163.
Buses from Gloucester, Stroud, Wotton-under-Edge, Cirencester
and Malmesbury (all infrequent).
Car parks in Tetbury.

The walk passes through Estcourt Park to Shipton Moyne, then along part of the Fosse Way and by field paths alongside the river Avon, through Easton Grey to Pinkney. The return is made through Westonbirt School grounds and Doughton.

The walk may be shortened by omitting Easton Grey and Pinkney. A short walk to Shipton Moyne returning through Doughton is also described.

TETBURY.   This is an interesting place. The Market House, built in 1655, is supported on stout stone pillars. The Priory, built in 1767, was part of a priory for Cistercian monks who later moved to Kingswood. The church is eighteenth-century with very large windows.

The walk starts at Northfields car park in The Chipping, by going down Chipping Steps to Cirencester Road. Here turn right and in a few yards bear right down a path with cattle pens on the left to cross the road at the foot of Gumstool Hill. Go along a track with sheep pens on the left and in 50 yards the track has a stream on the right. Continue for 200 yards to a Y junction. Take the left fork, away from the stream, the path leading to the road to the old railway station. Turn right to the Tetbury-Malmesbury road (A434). Turn left along the road for 10 yards, then turn down a track on the right. In 50 yards this bears left, with a house and stream on the right. Go along the track and where this turns left into the sewage works go ahead through a gate (opposite a ruined cottage) into a field, keeping to the wall on the left. Go over a wooden stile, through three fields with the boundary on the left, crossing two stone stiles, to a gate and stile on to a track. Cross this and go over the fence into a field with a wall and hedge on the right. The path follows approximately the right-hand field boundary for some 300 yards to a wooden stile into a field with the hedge on the right. After 60 yards turn right through a gate in the hedge towards a stream. Turn left up the side of the stream to cross a low stone bridge. Almost immediately turn left over a wooden bridge and go straight ahead up the field for some 400 yards. The path is not visible on the ground, but keep direction from the line of the bridge. Ignore the gates on the right. As the top of the rise is reached, a track will be seen coming in on the left. Cross a single strand of barbed wire ahead (a hooked handle is provided to help you) and go forward on to the track. You are now in **Estcourt Park**, where turn right along the metalled road.

In about a quarter of a mile go over a cross-track to a cattle grid ahead. Continue straight ahead ignoring the track on the left. (This leads to the sixteenth-century stable block, the mansion having been demolished some years ago.) Cross a second cattle grid with a house on the right. At this point look half-right to see a gate into a field some 60 yards away. Now look for a landmark on the field boundary beyond, as you must go through the gate, crossing the field diagonally in the direction in which you are now looking, to a stone stile in the wall, giving access to the next field. This may be ploughed. Keeping the same direction as before, go through a line of trees until a gate is seen ahead. Go through, crossing the field in the same direction to join a track leading to a farm. At the farm turn right in the direction of the church and go over a stile which is by a gate. The path goes through two fields to enter the churchyard at **Shipton Moyne.** Note the house on the left as you cross the first field. This is Hodges Barn, a house converted from a barn. The domed roofs are dovecotes and the structure is probably sixteenth-century. Leave the churchyard by the main gate, going along the lane to the road. The various routes diverge here (**1**).

SHIPTON MOYNE. The church was rebuilt in the nineteenth century. It contains an Italian-style pulpit, a number of fourteenth-century effigies, and the Estcourt Chapel with seventeenth-century effigies surrounded by wrought iron railings.
The inn has the unusual name of the Cat and Custard Pot.

From the church turn left along the road, then left at the next junction (along the Malmesbury road). In about 50 yards turn right along a track signposted 'Public bridleway', which continues for three quarters of a mile to a T junction. (Ignore the track on the right after about half a mile). Turn right along a lane which is part of the Roman Fosse Way from Bath to Lincoln. In about half a mile cross the Malmesbury-Old Sodbury road (B4040) and continue on the Fosse Way along a gravel track for some 400 yards, then through a gate ahead and along a green lane for another quarter-mile. At the end of the lane go through a gate into a field and alongside the hedge on the left to cross a stone bridge over the Bristol Avon river. This is a delightful place to linger. Turn right up a sunken track for 100 yards, through the gate ahead and alongside the hedge on the right. Go through two gates a short distance apart, then past a derelict farm on the right. Go ahead over a wide bridge, through a gate and forward for 50 yards to a path bearing left between hedges into a field with a hedge on the left. Go the length of the field (ignore the first gate on the left), turning left at the field corner through a gate. Immediately turn right along an obvious track, keeping to the right-hand hedge. The

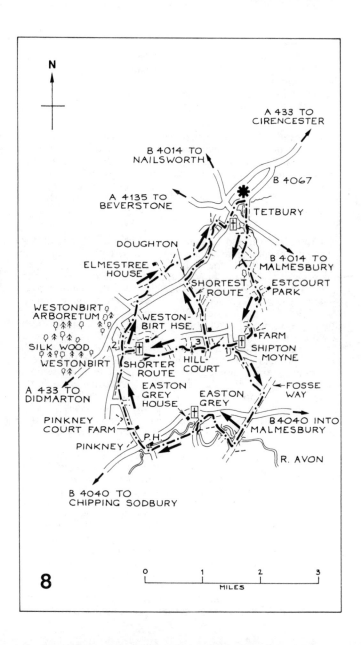

N

A 433 TO CIRENCESTER

B 4014 TO NAILSWORTH

B 4067

A 4135 TO BEVERSTONE

TETBURY

DOUGHTON

B 4014 TO MALMESBURY

ELMESTREE HOUSE

SHORTEST ROUTE

ESTCOURT PARK

WESTONBIRT ARBORETUM

WESTON-BIRT HSE.

FARM

SILK WOOD

SHIPTON MOYNE

WESTONBIRT

SHORTER ROUTE

HILL COURT

A 433 TO DIDMARTON

EASTON GREY HOUSE

EASTON GREY

FOSSE WAY

PINKNEY COURT FARM

B 4040 INTO MALMESBURY

PINKNEY

P.H.

R. AVON

B 4040 TO CHIPPING SODBURY

8

0   1   2   3
MILES

track bears left and then right to a gate and across a field to a gate
on the B4040 road. Turn left and in 10 yards turn half-left along a
minor road to a T junction. This is **Easton Grey.** Turn right and
the entrance to the church is on the left. Ahead is the drive to the
manor-house. The route is through the village by turning left,
down the hill to the river bridge.

EASTON GREY. The church was rebuilt in the mid nineteenth
     century and has a Jacobean pulpit. The adjacent manor is
     Georgian. The facade is best seen from the bridge over the Avon.
     As one descends the village, on the right is the mill, now a
     house; below on the left is Bridge House, restored in the
     seventeenth century, its formal gardens being visible from the
     bridge.

   Cross the river and go along the road for 100 yards, then go
through the first gate on the right, up a path between trees
(ignore the path on the right) in the direction of tall trees,
crossing the field to bring a wood, with the river below, on the
right. Look right as you cross the field to see the manor. Cross a
stile near the field corner and in 100 yards the hedge turns right
but the path bears half-left away from the river. Go ahead over
the crest of the field and descend to cross a wooden stile in the
field corner, with a hedge and the river on the right. Go along
this hedge and fence until reaching a stile about 20 yards to the
left of the field corner. Over the stile go along by the fence on the
right to farm buildings. Now go round the buildings keeping
them on the right. Past the last building go ahead to a gate into a
lane. Turn right for 100 yards to a metalled lane, where turn left,
following the lane over the river bridge to the B4040 road at
crossroads at **Pinkney.** The walk will continue along the road
opposite. The Eagle inn is on the right, where refreshments may
be obtained if required.
   From the inn go back to the crossroads, turning right along the
road for about one mile, passing Pinkney Court Farm on the
right. Where the road turns left go through a gate ahead, across
the farmyard in the same direction, and then continue alongside
the hedge on the left. Go through a gate, alongside the hedge,
but where this turns left go forward, bearing slightly left to the
field corner near the road. Cross a fence and along the field side
(road on left) to a stile on the left at the next corner giving access
to the road. Turn right and cross the road coming in on the right
to go through a hunting gate ahead, along the field side, with the
road on the left. Go through a hunting gate, along the side of a
narrow meadow and out at a gate to pass in front of a house.
Enter the gate ahead and go along a path with a fence on the left
and trees and golf course on the right. The path leads to the road

at the eastern end of **Westonbirt** village. Note the drive immediately opposite up which you will go to continue the walk. To visit the church and see Westonbirt House turn right along the metalled drive.

WESTONBIRT. The village was built by the architect of Westonbirt House, being moved to its present site before the house was built. The house, built between 1863 and 1870, is now a girls' school and not open to the public, though you will walk through the grounds. The church is adjacent to the house and contains memorials to the Holford family who owned the Westonbirt estate. On the opposite side of the Tetbury-Didmarton road (A433) is the Westonbirt Arboretum and Silk Wood — open to the public and particularly enjoyable in spring and autumn.

(2) From the church gate go along the metalled drive, through a gate and in 50 yards turn right up a drive with a cattle grid and a lodge on the right (marked 'Private road'). In a quarter of a mile a cross-track will be reached, affording an excellent view of Westonbirt House. Cross the track and continue in the same direction as before (there is a small wood on the right near the start of the path) to go through a metal gate beside a wooden one and on to a wooden gate ahead (ignore the gate half-left). Continue to a metal gate at the crossroads near the Hare and Hounds hotel.

Diagonally over the crossroads (which are extremely busy) go through a small gate and in a few yards a second gate into a field. A gate will be seen in the fence ahead (ignore the white gate to the right of a house). Go to this and across the next field in the same general direction to go through a white gate. Turn approximately half-right to a gate some 100 yards from the field corner, then cross the next field diagonally to a stone stile halfway up the left-hand hedge of the field. Continue across the next field to go over a stone stile in the top corner. Now turn half-right with a wall then a hedge on the right. Go through a gap in the wall ahead and along the next field with a hedge on the right, crossing the next wall by means of a hunting stile. Cross the field bearing slightly left to go over a bar stile in the fence ahead. Go slightly right to cross the drive leading to Elmestree House on the left. *(From here the route may be diverted. At the time of going to press, the paths were still in use, but any diversions will be clearly marked. The object of these diversions is to provide Highgrove House, home of the Prince and Princess of Wales, with greater privacy.)* Go through the gate ahead, with trees, house and pond on the right, then through a second gate bearing half-right to go through a small gate at the field corner, with a wall on the right. Highgrove House is on the right. Continue across the next field in the same direction to a narrow wood, where there is a stone stile almost blocked by a large tree.

The path goes between walls for about 100 yards and out through
a gate. (In summer this path will be impassable because of
nettles, but a bar stile can be used to the left of the stile by the
tree, then crossing the field to a gate just to the left of the gate
mentioned above.) Turn right down the side of the field to a
stone stile but do not cross. Turn left with the hedge on the right.
This bears left then right. In the field corner cross a stone stile
and go along the edge of the field (ploughed) with a wall on the
right and over a stone stile. Cross the field diagonally aiming
towards bungalows with Tetbury church spire just to the right,
and crossing a small stream before going over a stone stile. *(Here
the proposed diversion joins the existing route.)* Continue in the
same direction to a stone stile with a bungalow on the right,
emerging on to a road. Turn right along the road, right at the
next junction and left along the main road (A433) to the town
centre of **Tetbury,** passing the church on the right.

The shorter route (7½ miles)

Follow the route to the end of the paragraph marked (1),
bringing you to Shipton Moyne.

Almost directly opposite the lane from the church a path goes
between buildings. Go over the stile and cross the field, bearing
very slightly right to a stile at a gap in the hedge. Cross the next
field to go through a gate just to the right of a small barn. Cross
the field to go over a stone stile just to the left of a gate. Continue
with a wall on the right to a stile into a road. The shortest route
diverges here (3).

Across the road, just on the right, is a stone stile with a wooden
fence. From the stile two gates can be seen, the first some 30 yards
from the left-hand field corner. Go across these two fields using
the gates and cross the next field to go out through a gate on the
right of a house. Follow the track, turning right by the second
cottage, then left round farm buildings. In 50 yards, turn right by
a stockyard. After about 50 yards turn left along a track, having a
building on the left but none on the right. (Ignore the drive to Hillcourt and two other entries on the left.) The track turns leftwards
and the front of **Hillcourt** will be seen on the left. The farm track
winds through an iron gate and leads to a gate between two small
woods. Go through and cross the field bearing slightly right past
the corner of the right-hand wood to a stone stile (not easily visible)
in the wall alongside a road.

Cross, go over a stone stile and straight ahead to a gate set at an
angle to the path. Go through and continue in a line at approximately 30 degrees to the fence (that is in the same direction
as before), making for a large cedar tree. At the tree turn roughly
half-right to go through a small iron gate in the fence ahead,
then diagonally down the field to a small gate in front of
Westonbirt House. Turn half-left to reach a gate at the car park

for the golf course. Continue forward to the drive where on the right will be seen a gate on the path leading to the church at **Westonbirt.**

Now continue the walk from the paragraph marked (2) in the long route.

Shortest route (5 miles)

Follow the long route to the end of the paragraph marked (1), then the shorter route to the end of the paragraph marked (3).

Turn right along the road for 500 yards to a junction. Cross and go down the track opposite, with a house on the right. The track is broad at first, then narrow and sometimes two paths a few yards apart. After half a mile go through a small gate on the left (there is a hunting gate opposite on the right) down a track with a wall on the left, over a bridge and through a gate on to a green lane. In half a mile this leads to the Tetbury-Didmarton road (A433), where turn right past the village of **Doughton.**

Go along the main road, noting the seventeenth-century manor-house on the right. Continue past the entrance drive and lodge (on the left) to Highgrove and in half a mile take the new footpath on the left, 30 yards past the road to Shipton Moyne, to a small stone cattle byre, where continue over the field towards the housing estate, with Tetbury church spire just to the right and crossing a small stream before going over a stone stile. Continue in the same direction to a stone stile with a bungalow on the right, emerging on to a road. Turn right along the road, right at the next junction and left along the main road (A433) to the town centre of **Tetbury**, passing the church on the right.

Walk 9	THE WINDRUSH VALLEY AND THE SLAUGHTERS

Circular walk from Bourton-on-the-Water via the river Windrush, Naunton, Eyford and the Slaughters (9 miles).
1-inch map no. 144. 2½-inch map sheet no. SP 12. 1:50,000 map no. 163
Pulham's bus service from Cheltenham (infrequent).
Ample car parking in Bourton-on-the-Water.

The walk follows the valley of the river Windrush upstream to Naunton, sometimes beside the stream, sometimes on the valley side. The return is made by walking over the hill into the river Eye valley, following the stream through wood, meadows and pleasant villages.

BOURTON-ON-THE-WATER is a busy and popular village. The village green forms the banks of the river Windrush which is spanned by a number of graceful low stone bridges. Beside the green are typical Cotswold-stone houses.

The church is not particularly notable except for the cupola on the eighteenth-century tower which contains a peal of bells on which hymn tunes are played at times. The fourteenth-century chancel ceiling is painted. There is a complete model of the village at the back of the Old New Inn. In the grounds of a lovely old house is Birdland, where exotic birds are kept in landscaped gardens which are open to the public.

Leave **Bourton-on-the-Water** village green, near the war memorial, turning left over the topmost river bridge. Go along the street until Harrington House is reached (this is a Holiday Fellowship Guest House, built in 1740, and a listed building). Opposite the large gates a footpath sign indicates a path between buildings. This leads to a kissing gate and across a field to the bank of the river Windrush. Continue along the riverside, with the river on the right, crossing a small bridge, until a low stone bridge is reached. Here turn right in front of a delightful mill house, to emerge on the main road into the village. Turn left along the pavement to the Fosse Way (A429), cross carefully and enter a pasture through an iron gate, with the river on the left. Cross the field, keeping the old railway embankment on the right, and enter a second field through a small metal gate at the corner (ignore the continuation of the first field on the left). Keep the hedge and fence on the left. The path rises slightly to a stile giving access to the disused Kingham-Cheltenham railway track. Walk 40 yards along the track to a path on the right between a copse and a fence. The path leaves the railway and shortly descends to a gate into a lane, dropping leftwards to another mill house with stables and riverside garden.

Continue up the lane to a T junction, turning right to Aston Farm. The path goes through the farm, between two new barns, into a field. The farmer has been kind enough to leave the path unploughed, so please keep to the path, which goes forward into a field with a wood on the right. (This is a bridle path and in wet weather, for a mile or so, is very muddy.) Keep the wood on the right as the path drops steeply. Go forward, ignoring the track under the railway arch on the left. Keep to the main track, ignoring paths either to left or right. Go through an iron gate into a field with a wood on the right. In 300 yards one is on a bank above the river, the path descending diagonally leftwards to continue along the riverside for approximately one mile, passing through one small gate and two large gates. Continue forward along the path until a gate is seen ahead, about 100 yards left from the river at **Lower Harford**, opening into a lane.

Go through the gate across the lane to a gap in the hedge 30 yards ahead, where turn left following the line of electricity poles

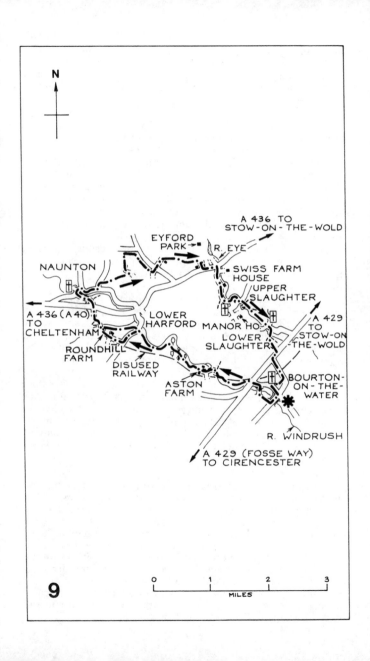

and aiming for a metal gate ahead. Continue up the valley (ignore gates on the right), through another metal gate just to the right of a pole, going forward with a stream on the right, to a wooden gate. Pass through, turning right to cross the stream by a stone slab bridge.

An alternative route to that in the previous paragraph is useful when grass is long near haytime. On reaching the lane at Lower Harford turn left up the hill for 700 yards. Just before reaching the old railway turn right along the track to Roundhill Farm. At the farm bear left round a garage, then along the side of the field with a wall and farm buildings on the right. This leads to stone steps into the next field. Keep to the wall on the right to go over a stone stile and forward descending to a wooden stile. Go forward again to cross a stream by the stone slab bridge mentioned in the previous paragraph.

Go diagonally leftwards up the hill on a path leading to an iron gate and continue on a track, with a wall on the right, to go through an iron gate on to the Andoversford to Stow-on-the-Wold road (A436).

Cross the road and go through a metal gate, turning half-left down a well-defined track. You now see the village of **Naunton** in the Windrush valley, surrounded by fields. The track leads to the road near the church. Whilst descending, look on the right for a square gabled building with a lean-to shed. This is a fifteenth-century dovecote with more than a thousand nest-holes.

NAUNTON. The church has been restored and contains a white stone pulpit, an old font and a few interesting memorials. On leaving the church turn left over the river. Past the first cottage on the right, look for an old cider press in excellent state of preservation (please remember that this is in a private entry). Continue along the road through the village to the Black Horse inn where refreshment may be obtained.

To continue the walk, from the inn turn right and take the first road on the right. Some 100 yards up the road, go through a wooden gate on the right, following a track up to a small wood. Go through the gates at each end of the wood, the path continuing across three fields (usually this path is unploughed). The path drops into a hollow and enters a hedged portion on the left leading up to a farm track, where continue forward with the hedge on the right to a lane by a garden wall, where turn right and follow the path along the side of two large fields, with the wall, then a fence on one's left, until reaching a pair of gates leading on to the road. (This is Buckle Street, an ancient way from Bourton to Broadway and beyond.)

Cross the road and proceed along a farm track until a barn is reached on the right. Here turn right along the track through a metal gate to follow a well-defined path ahead through three fields, continuing through a gate into a field with a wall on the right. At the bottom of the hill turn half-right to reach the Naunton-Stow road (A436) by some cottages. This is **Eyford.**

EYFORD. The house in Eyford Park was built in 1910 on the site of a former mansion. The lodge which you will pass on the left along the road dates from 1870.

Turn left along this busy road for some 500 yards, facing on-coming traffic as there is no footpath. Turn right at the first lane, marked 'Swiss Farm House', with the river Eye on the left. At the first junction bear right. The lane, level at first, climbs through a wood. In spring the river banks below are a delight with kingcups. Follow the lane to a house on the left, passing through a gate into a field in front of the house and leaving by a wicket gate ahead. Go down the field in the same direction, through a gate and along a track (sometimes muddy) which leads to **Upper Slaughter**. Note the ford and stone bridge ahead on the left; we shall return to these but follow the track turning right into the village.

UPPER SLAUGHTER. It is said that the name derives from 'sloe-tree', of which there are a number in the district. The side entrance to the church is on the right just beyond the school. The church has a Norman tower and a fine arch leading from the tower into the church. It is unusual in having two fonts, one a copy of the Tudor original. Part of the manor-house is fifteenth-century but the front facing the road is Elizabethan. To see this, go forward from the main entrance of the church to the road and turn right for about 100 yards to a junction, where turn left for 150 yards to the manor entrance on the left.

Return to the ford, cross the bridge and turn right with cottages on the left. At the next road junction go left up the hill until the road turns sharp left. An iron gate will be found on the right; pass through and go diagonally right across the field to a kissing gate. Views are obtained on the right of the back of the manor-house. The path goes forward to a wicket gate, where bear half-right to another gate and footbridge. Continue with the river on the right to the wall by the mill dam at **Lower Slaughter**. In spring you may see a swan's nest on the opposite bank, as there is usually a pair of swans swimming majestically up and down. The path goes through a gate just to the left of the mill buildings into a lane, where turn right to arrive on the river side with the mill and water wheel on the right. This was grinding corn for the bakery (now the post office) up to a few years ago. Walk alongside the river to the small village green.

LOWER SLAUGHTER. This is a lovely village with bridges over the river Eye and an old fountain on the green. The church and manor-house are on the left of the river. The church was rebuilt in the nineteenth century. The manor-house is seventeenth-century, whilst the dovecote in the grounds is sixteenth-century and one of the largest in Gloucestershire.

Follow the river until it turns right, away from the road. Here a tarred path should be followed, with the river on the right. Shortly the river turns left under the path which continues forward across two fields to the Fosse Way (A429). Cross with care, turn right along the pavement and left at the first road junction. Walk through new housing for a quarter of a mile to Bourton Vale School on the right. On the left of the school grounds is a path, entered over a stone stile, leading towards the church. At the junction with a cross-path turn right, then shortly left to reach the road by the church, where a left turn will bring the walker back to the village green at **Bourton-on-the-Water.**

Walk 10	OVER THE DOWNS
	NEAR MORETON-IN-MARSH

Circular walk from Moreton-in-Marsh through Batsford to Blockley, returning via Bourton-on-the-Hill and Sezincote (9½, 8, or 5½ miles).
1-inch map no. 144. 2½-inch map sheet no. SP 13: 1:50,000 map no. 151.
Midland Red bus service from Evesham to Blockley and Moreton; Pulham's bus service from Cheltenham to Moreton (both infrequent).
Car parking in Moreton and Blockley.

The walk goes through fields to Batsford Park and church, then over Blockley Downs to Blockley. The return is made over the Downs to Bourton-on-the-Hill, through Sezincote Park and fields to Moreton-in-Marsh.

The walk may be shortened by omitting Blockley and further shortened by omitting Batsford church and Blockley.

MORETON-IN-MARSH is a pleasant large village on the Fosse Way. It has a broad High Street planted with trees. In the centre of the High Street is the Redesdale Market Hall, a mock Tudor building of the nineteenth century. Opposite, on the corner of

Oxford Street, is the sixteenth-century Curfew Tower, probably the oldest building in the village.

Starting from the Market Hall in **Moreton-in-Marsh** and going in the direction of Stratford, take the first road on the left (ladies' toilets on left) which in 100 yards leads to Hospital Road. Cross and go through a wicket gate (to the left of large gates) and in 20 yards go over a stile into a field with a short fence on the left. Taking a line from this fence go forward for 350 yards to a concealed stile in the hedge on the left, about 100 yards beyond power cables. (The path is faintly visible on the ground and wanders a little from a straight line.) Go over the stile, keeping the same general direction, for 50 yards to cross a poor footbridge at a disused wicket gate, 25 yards left from the right-hand field corner. Go ahead for 120 yards to pass through a wicket gate and across the next field to go over a wooden stile. Beyond this field may be ploughed, but cross in the same direction for 300 yards to go through a wicket gate 50 yards to the left of the far right-hand field corner. Go ahead for 200 yards to pass through a line of trees and a further 150 yards to a wicket gate by a farm gate in the field corner, with a long thin copse on the right. Bear slightly right alongside the copse. In 25 yards cross a stream, ignoring the gate on the right (there is no footbridge but the fence on the right is very useful). Keep alongside the copse on the right and in 200 yards go through a wooden farm gate at a gap in the copse, bearing left round a group of trees for 50 yards to another farm gate. Continue along the side of the hedge on the right, through an iron wicket gate and in 100 yards there is a wall on the right. This is the corner of **Batsford Park.** The shortest route diverges here **(1).**
  Turn right through a wooden hunting gate and in a few yards go through a second one. Keep alongside the wall on the left for about three-quarters of a mile, passing through four fields and having a good view of **Batsford House** in the park. 20 yards before the far corner of the fourth field is reached, go through a wooden gate on the left into a field and alongside the fence on the right. Go over the fence ahead into the next field, then forward for about 100 yards over further fences to a wooden gate to emerge on to a minor road. Turn left for 100 yards up the road, then left for 400 yards along a road lined with lime trees to **Batsford Church.**

BATSFORD PARK AND CHURCH. The house is late nineteenth-century and in the Cotswold-Elizabethan style. The gardens were made by Lord Redesdale and ornamented with Buddhas and a Chinese temple.
  The church was rebuilt in 1860. It contains a stone pulpit, a wooden enclosed pew at the rear and a number of monuments.

From the church turn left along the road and in 50 yards take the left fork at a Y junction. On the left along the road is the magnificent gatehouse and the stables. In 200 yards turn left at crossroads and go up the hill until the road turns sharp left. The shorter route diverges here (2).

On the right-hand side of the road take the signposted path going half-left, crossing the field (which may be ploughed) to the far corner and giving good views of Northwick Park and House. Go through a small wooden gate and along the side of the field (which may be ploughed) with trees on the right. At the next corner, ignore two obvious gates to the left but continue through a narrow part of the field, with a wall on the left, to a small wooden gate. This entry may be rather overgrown. Keep to the wall on the left (over the wall is an old track completely overgrown); on the right are views over Blockley and Northwick Park. After 300 yards the path bears slightly right, then bears right downhill with a wall or fence on the left. The path leads through a small wooden gate and, still keeping to the hedge on the left, go to an iron gate on to a gravel track. Turn left and in 600 yards this track leads to the road in the village of **Blockley.** Note this place as you will return here. Turn right, passing Lower Brook House hotel on the right and in 200 yards turn left up a tarred path to the church.

BLOCKLEY is a large Cotswold village, some of the houses dating from the seventeenth century.

The church contains Norman work and there is a contribution from each succeeding century. On the south wall of the chancel is a beautiful piscina (basin) and sedilia (group of three seats). There are two important brasses, one on the floor before the altar, the other on the wall beside the sedilia. The church has numerous monuments to the Northwick family who resided at Northwick Park.

The mansion in the park dates from the seventeenth century and once contained a famous collection of pictures.

Turn left at the church entrance for the High Street and the Crown Inn where refreshments may be obtained.

To continue the walk, from the church entrance go up the road and across the village green to the war memorial, the old mill-pond being on the right. At the memorial turn right and at the bottom of the hill turn right again. Continue along the road and 50 yards beyond the lane by which you entered Blockley turn left up a short grassy track leading into a field through an iron gate (the right-hand one of two). Keep near to the hedge on the left and through the gate ahead. Go up the field for 150 yards to an entry just to the right of Blockley Park Farm. On the right are the remains of an old fish-pond and looking back gives an excellent view of Blockley

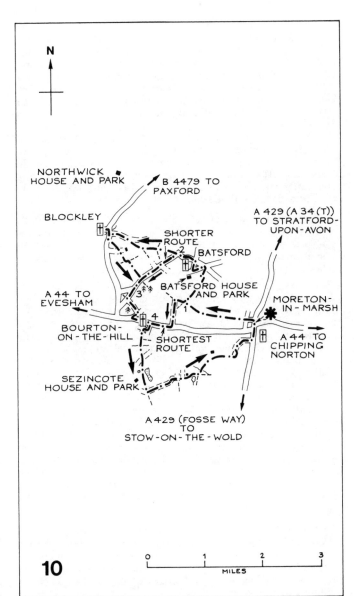

N

NORTHWICK
HOUSE AND PARK

B 4479 TO
PAXFORD

A 429 (A 34 (T))
TO STRATFORD-
UPON-AVON

BLOCKLEY

SHORTER
ROUTE

BATSFORD

A 44 TO
EVESHAM

BATSFORD HOUSE
AND PARK

MORETON-
IN-MARSH

BOURTON-
ON-THE-HILL

SHORTEST
ROUTE

A 44 TO
CHIPPING
NORTON

SEZINCOTE
HOUSE AND PARK

A 429 (FOSSE WAY)
TO
STOW-ON-THE-WOLD

10

0   1   2   3
MILES

church. Through the entry by the farm immediately turn right through a gate into a field with a fence on the left. Go up the field 400 yards to go through an iron gate in the left-hand corner on to a track. Turn left for 200 yards between trees and through an iron gate. Immediately turn right through a hunting gate into a field with a wall and trees on the right. Keep to the right-hand field boundary through two fields, then go through a wooden gate and a copse to a road. Turn right along the road for a quarter of a mile to a Y junction.

(3) Ignore the right fork and in 300 yards take the first track on the left with a wire fence on the left. In 200 yards there is a wood on the right concealing old quarries. In another 100 yards ignore the track going off right but go through the gate ahead for 350 yards, then turn right along a track to a road. Here turn left down the road into **Bourton-on-the-Hill**.

BOURTON-ON-THE-HILL. The church is not notable but has Norman pillars supporting the south arcade. It contains two unusual objects — Standard Winchester Bushel and Peck measures made in bell metal. Down the road on the right is an old manor-house, fifteenth-century tithe barn and dovecote.

(4) To continue, go down the road from the church, taking the first road on the right and right again at the next junction. In 25 yards turn left up a narrow lane opposite a gate into a garden. The lane goes between buildings and, looking back, one has a view of an attractive garden with the church behind. In 100 yards the lane ends at a gate. Go through and keep to the wall on the right to pass through a gate and across a long field (220 yards) to a gate into a field with a hedge on the left. After 200 yards go through trees ahead and forward for 150 yards to a small wooden gate, then through a narrow belt of trees to a second gate. You are now in **Sezincote Park**. Go straight ahead, between small copses across a drive and straight ahead for 300 yards to a path just visible to the right of tall trees with a fence on the left. The path leads to a wooden gate. On going through, there is a pond on either side and in 10 yards a second gate. Cross the next field in the same direction. On the right is **Sezincote House,** and over to the left a large lake. In 200 yards go through a gate, then continue over the brow of the hill for 400 yards to the far corner of the field and a metalled drive.

SEZINCOTE HOUSE was built in 1805 in Indian style by Sir Charles Cockerell of the East India Company and was the inspiration for the Brighton Pavilion. The main block is faced with orange-coloured stone said to have been stained to give the correct Indian tone. The landscaped gardens are not visible from the path.

To continue, turn left passing a house on the left, and follow the metalled drive for just over half a mile until it turns left into Upper Rye Farm. Here go straight ahead, with a fence on the left, then through a gate with barns on the left and along a track towards a wood. The track bears left at the wood to a gate on the right. Go through and round the end of the wood to a gate. Cross the next field half-left for 200 yards and go through a gate between tall trees and over a stream. Go alongside the right-hand fence for 250 yards to a gate into a field with the hedge 50 yards to the left. The path crosses the field 250 yards to the far left-hand corner. Ignore the track going left to the farm but go ahead through a gate and alongside the hedge on the left. At the next boundary, go through a gate and along the hedge on the left. In a quarter of a mile ignore the gate jutting out perpendicular to the hedge but go through the gate 80 yards ahead on the track towards Dunstall Farm. In 100 yards turn left over a stile beside an iron gate and along the side of a field with a fence on the right and in 200 yards cross a narrow piece of rough ground. Ignore a gate on the right and from this point cross the field diagonally to the far left-hand corner to go through a gateway into a lane which may be rather overgrown. Shortly pass houses on the right, then the lane turns right passing ambulance and fire stations. On reaching the main road (A429) turn left to **Moreton-in-Marsh.**

The shorter route (8 miles)

Follow the long route to the end of the paragraph marked (2).

Turn left along the road, with Batsford Park on the left. In 1 mile a Y junction is reached. Now go to the paragraph marked (3) in the long route.

The shortest route (5½ miles)

Follow the long route to the end of the paragraph marked (1).

Continue forward, with the wall and **Batsford Park** and house on the right. In 300 yards a gate is reached giving access to a drive by a lodge. Turn left along the drive for half a mile to the Moreton-Broadway road (A44). Turn right and in a quarter of a mile there is the manor-house and the tithe barn on the left. In a further 300 yards you will reach the church at **Bourton-on-the-Hill.** Now continue the walk from the paragraph marked (4) in the long route.

INDEX OF PLACES

Printed by C. I. Thomas & Sons (Haverfordwest) Ltd., Press Buildings,
Merlin's Bridge, Haverfordwest, Pembrokeshire.